Forgive Us
Our Digressions

Forgive Us Our Digressions

AN AUTOBIOGRAPHY

Jim and Henny Backus

ST. MARTIN'S PRESS · NEW YORK

Design by Debby Jay

    Library of Congress Cataloging-in-Publication Data

Backus, Jim.
     Forgive us our digressions / by Jim and Henny Backus.
        p.   cm.
     "A Thomas Dunne book."
     ISBN 0-312-01529-1 : $15.95
     1. Backus, Jim.   2. Backus, Henny.   3. Actors—
United States—Biography.   I. Backus, Henny.
II. Title.
PN2287.B14A3 1988
792'.028'0924—dc19
[B]   87-27346

First Edition

10 9 8 7 6 5 4 3 2 1

To KATHY J. SEGAL
and JOEL PRESTON
. . . without whom there would be no book

Contents

Photo sections follow pages 82 and 114.

Foreword

If you want to know why Jim Backus grew up to be Thurston Howell III, read *Forgive Us Our Digressions* and meet Dear Old Dad and Jim's mother, who was a facsimile of Billie Burke, complete with small dog on lap. The dog had to be removed surgically.

Over the years I have watched Jim and Henny's great romance blossom as they grew together. Theirs has been a life of madness, productive artistic pursuits, parties, and a headlong Noel Cowardian existence. These people are both totally bleeped and they don't know it. Henny thinks everybody swims a mile a day and plays solitaire with a marked deck. Jim took up fencing last year instead of installing a security system. You've heard of off-the-wall? Jim and Henny *are* the wall.

I love the book and I love you, Henny and Jim.

As George Burns said, "I laughed and I cried."

Phyllis Diller

Preface

This Is Henny. . . .

My husband Jimmy is sloppy, disorganized, vague, preoc-
cupied, distraught, and undisciplined. He's also the most
meticulously confused person I've ever met. Yet he arrives
at his destination in life as if it were carefully charted. . . .
But I love him, and I always have. I love him, but I don't
understand him.

Maybe after you read this book you can explain him to
me. Who knows? Maybe you'll love him, too.

This Is Jim. . . .

George Burns wrote the Foreword for our last book, *Backus
Strikes Back*. And a very good foreword it was. I asked
George what was the difference between a preface and a
foreword. "A preface is a foreword handled by an agent,"
he said with typical Burns acumen and finality. When George
gives you an answer, that's it! It's finished, closed, ended,
kaput. So that's the reason I'm writing the preface for this
book and George is having soup.

Actually, in his foreword, George said, "I loved this book.
It made me laugh and it made me cry, and it made me buy
a dictionary. It's a very good dictionary, but it has a very
bad foreword."

We're glad he liked our last book. It's one of the reasons
for this new one.

Actually, *Backus Strikes Back* was the story of a disease
and a misdiagnosis and how it affected me. At the end of

the book I said to Henny, "What if they made another mistake and I really do have Parkinson's? What'll I do?"

"Write a sequel," she said.

And here it is.

Forgive Us
Our Digressions

Dear Old Dad

Where was I? Oh, yeah, back on the couch . . . or rather, the chair. After so many years of it you can get pretty relaxed about the whole thing. Anyway, the fifty minutes were almost up. I could barely see the clock, which he had stashed behind the picture of Karl Menninger. He kept hiding it in different places. Finding the clock was "my thing." It was bad enough to have to come here three times a week. That was nothing. . . . Back in New York it was six times a week . . . every day but Sunday. But then it was only eight bucks a session. Imagine that! And all my New York Freudian lady ever said to me was hello when I started with her and good-bye when I left to come to Hollywood. They didn't talk to you back then. You had to pull it out of your own head, and Dr. Sybil Stern was a genuine New York Freudian. She had the official black leather couch and the authorized Picasso prints. She even had the collection of pre-Columbian sculptures. And I used to have a hell of a job balancing that heavy rock crystal ashtray on my sternum. Yes, I smoked. Everybody smoked. I used to knock off five or six during the psychoanalysis session. That's all it was ever called in those days, psychoanalysis. Not your piss-elegant "therapy."

1

"Piss-elegant." That was one of the few profanities my mother used. For example, Clara Outin was piss-elegant; Nora Feebach was not. Simple? Her only other vehement word was "shit-ass." Hitler was a shit-ass; Churchill was not. This from my blond, beautiful, elegant mother. One thing she would never do was use the name of the Lord in vain. Come to think of it, lately I've cut that out, too. My cop-out agnosticism has been wearing pretty thin ever since my last birthday—a big one! I figured I would know the answer to "Is there or isn't there" soon enough. I ration myself nowadays to a few well-placed "schmucks."* It's a very handy word, believe me.

My beautiful mother was, of all things, a rabbi-groupie. She loved to hear them talk on the radio. Compared to them, Reverend Peacock was a shit-ass. My father, considering his Mayflower background, was completely free of racial or religious prejudice. When I informed him that I intended to marry Henny (whom he adored), he took an extra long sip on his Canadian Club and said, "I hope you know what you're doing." Then he took another tug and thought for a moment. "On the other hand, I hear they make great wives. . . . They don't drink . . . save your money . . . and have great boobs." Only on the first and last counts was he right!

I keep thinking of the last time I saw my father. He was talking about getting old. He had retired and, much as he loved the Florida life, missed the hustle and bustle of Cleveland and his business. The last years of his life he lived in Reddington Beach, Florida. I recall sitting on the deck with him some twenty feet from the Gulf. It was sunset. We had just come from playing golf and were sipping on two tall ones. It was that quiet time just before the sun, looking

---

*"Schmuck": A woman says to her husband, "You're a schmuck! You're a schmuck's schmuck! If they had a contest for schmucks, you'd come in second!"

"Why not first?" he asks.

"Because you're a schmuck!"

like a fluorescent wafer, took its plunge into the horizon. He took a tug on his pipe and said, "I'm going to miss this." The way he said it—no rancor, no fear, no "Why me?" Just, "I'm going to miss this. . . ." He once said, "Jimmy, if something good is happening to you, if you're on a great roll, stop! Stop and look at it. Relish it. Enjoy the hell out of it; let it sink in. Put it in your memory bank."

This is exactly what G.L., that wise old shrink, told me years before. Only he described these memories as tapes. There were good tapes and bad tapes. The theory of the tapes is helping to bring me a smidgen of serenity . . . with room for lots more.

My father failed to see anything funny about the "golden years," as do I. I remember in the days of radio there was a show, *The Life of Reilly*, with a character called Digger O'Dell, a mortician. A smash! He killed the people! See what I mean? It's easy. You can make up those jokes without even trying, and you can do the same thing with senior citizens. Just mention bran . . . delirious! Prunes? . . . absolute pandemonium! Inability to make the facilities in time? . . . guaranteed tops in colon comedy! Couples going on second honeymoons and checking into the same room they had fifty years ago? . . . that's another must. Just the tag lines will suffice: "Just because you rented the ballroom doesn't mean you have to dance"; "This time I was the one who went into the bathroom and cried"; "Comes the sexual revolution and here I am with no ammunition!"

It's true, I've discovered, that older folks do have trouble remembering what happened yesterday, but we can remember what happened forty or fifty years ago with tunnel clarity. I was looking through several scrapbooks and discovered some rather startling facts. There were four or five pictures of TV shows that I vaguely remember making in the past ten years. I was unable to recall the director, the cast, or even the studio that made them. The further back the scrapbooks went, the more things seemed to sort themselves out. Maybe there is a section of the brain that

handles "things remembered." Maybe it has its own elim-
ination department, a sort of sit-com catharsis. I have made
more than two hundred pictures and television shows, and
I can't identify more than forty or fifty, let alone their plots
or cast. As for chronological order, forget it! There was
one still picture of our cast of *Ice Palace*—Richard Burton;
a lovely lady named Martha Hyers, who is now Mrs. Hal
Wallis; that super girl, the late Carolyn Jones; a fine little
actress named Shirley Knight—but as for the forty other
people, I drew a blank. Oh, yes, there was Robert Ryan, and
I finally recalled the name of the makeup man, Lee Green-
wood. I looked at some more stills. The same was true.

Then something weird happened. The class picture of
the third grade of Bratenahl School in Cleveland fell out.
What was it doing there in the first place? Twilight Zone
time! I remembered that we posed under an apple tree.
That was Bratenahl. In Beverly Hills for the class picture
they go on location. To give the photo a little action, Miss
McGee had the class watching Sidney Morton and me playing a game of mumbly-peg. It all came back. The smell of
apple blossoms . . . the soft spring air. There we were and,
so help me God, I was able to identify each and every one
of them—Hunter Van Sicklin, Elissa Strong, Walter Pratt,
Minnie Tomkins, Gorman Dawes, Janet Moss, Edith Sheridan, Charles Tomkins, Pearus Hasse, Corning Chisholm,
Ruby Hawkins, Sidney Morton, Helen Johnson. . . . There
we were—frozen in time under the apple tree.

I was in Cleveland not too long ago. They were having
a "local boy" celebration, and the papers sent a photographer with me as I visited the scenes of my childhood.
The apple tree was still there. And I sat at my old desk in
the second-grade classroom. It was pretty much the same
—the flag, the bust of George Washington, even that odor
peculiar to all schoolrooms—an acrid tang composed of
chalk, sweat, and damp corduroy. It's as identifiable in its
way as the smell of a new car. What I am driving at is that
I remember the room the way it looked and smelled more

than half a century ago. That's a lot of years. Damn near
threescore. But I couldn't remember a mere half score ago.
But who's keeping score? I wonder what a schoolroom today smells like.

Bratenahl, with a population of some fourteen hundred
people, was a tiny borough running along the shores of
Lake Erie and surrounded by Cleveland on all sides—a
stubborn little duchy that wanted and got complete au-
tonomy. It was said to be the richest village per capita in
the world. So what were *we* doing there? We had to be
there—somehow—or my socially ambitious mother would
have died!

The huge estates were for the most part on the boulevard
that fronted the lake, while on the other side of the boulevard were the residences of the butlers, the cooks, the
head gardeners, and the chauffeurs. All you ever had to say
was, "Which side of the boulevard?" and you knew. That
way they felt that everything was pigeonholed and in its
proper place.

While we weren't among the Cleveland "haves"—like
the Bradleys, who owned, among other things, the Cleveland Indians; the Gliddens, who had Glidden Paint; or the
Hannas, who owned the whole town (there were the Hanna
Steamship Line, the Hanna Theatre, the *Cleveland News*,
etc.)—still we were not exactly "have-nots." And while
we weren't in one of the lake estates, we were also not
on the other side of the boulevard. My father was a me-
chanical engineer, a graduate of Stevens Institute of Tech-
nology, and president of his own company, R. G. Backus
and Co. Heavy machinery. If it was at least a block long,
he made it.

Bratenahl School was unique in that it averaged a total
of only about a hundred kids in all eight grades. The prog-
eny of the rich and the children of their servants all went
there. It was a great school. Not a day goes by that I don't
use something I learned at Bratenahl School. (Incidentally,
one of my teachers was Margaret Hamilton, who later

became a well-known movie actress, the wicked witch of Oz.)

Altogether, Bratenahl was an ideal place in which to grow up—no crime and no business, unless you counted the chits at the country club, which was simply called "The Country Club"—no "Burning Bush" or "Hound Hollow." It was just the plain old Country Club. We were members (or my mother would have died!). I used to caddy there for thirty-five cents a loop.

Whenever I read a biography, I either skip, skim, or wade through the chapters dealing with the childhood. I don't know about you, but I find them boring. So we're going to take the liberty of dispensing with any mention of "how deep the snow was," "Uncle Charlie's booming laugh," "the gold watch that dangled from Daddy's vest," "Grandma's cookie cutter," "how the turkey seemed fit to burst," and "dipping her braids in the inkwell." Frankly, most of my childhood bored the hell out of me, and I'm sure it would most readers. I could hardly wait for puberty so I could get on with it. I know that your schooldays are supposed to be the happiest days of your life, but most of mine were just plain dull.

I guess part of my attitude is my fault because it wasn't until I was completely grown that I realized what an amusing and colorful person my father was. Up until he left us a few years ago, he was very young in appearance and outlook. And he had, to the end, one of the greatest senses of humor we've ever encountered.

My dad, Russell Gould Backus, was very successful as far back as I can remember. As I mentioned before, he was a graduate of Stevens, a brilliant engineer, and a master salesman, and the firm later called Backus and Spencer is still going strong in Cleveland, Ohio. Though a fairly wealthy man, Pop was an arch-conservative about money. In our parlance, he would have been called a cagey man with a buck. Being the cautious man he was, he took a very dim view of my wanting to become an actor.

Pop said all people connected with show business, especially actors, "didn't have their sails set." He was convinced that if he could spare the time, he could put the whole thing on a more organized basis. I'm afraid he was of the "actors are churls, louts, oafs, vagabonds, thieves, harlots, and shouldn't be allowed to vote or own property" school of thought. It wasn't until I was doing pretty well, particularly in television, that he did an about-face. He felt television was solid because it was endorsed by such Gibraltar-like names as General Motors, Du Pont, and Alcoa Aluminum.

When I was just starting in pictures and would write, for example, that I had a small part in a Warner Brothers movie, he would reply, "If it's not too late, son, get them to make your picture with Twentieth Century-Fox. They just went up five points on the Big Board." He would also forward me advice like, "Son, go with RKO. That Hughes fellow is a great engineer, and if anything goes wrong with his picture, you can always work in his plant."

My sweet grandmother, who was a very old lady at the time, was my number-one fan during my New York radio period. She used to listen every night for the sound of my voice. My father was one of those people who read and listened absentmindedly at the same time, unless it was a program he particularly wanted to hear. So, for example, if Rudy Vallee was singing a number, my grandmother would say, "Russell, is that Jimmy?" My father, without looking up from his paper, would mutter, "I guess so. He didn't write and say it wasn't." The answer would be the same whether it was Singin' Sam, Boake Carter, or Father Coughlin.

When I got my first really important part on radio, I wired my father to listen. I told him the name of the program and said to be sure to tune in. "It is Wednesday night at eight-thirty your time, on CBS." At the end of the week I got a note from him which said: "Loved the show and you were fine, but you were wrong, son, it was Tuesday night."

In 1948, our second year in Hollywood, Dad and Daisy, my mother, decided to visit us. Pop was in for a shock, as the last time he'd been here was in 1903. With Pop, things didn't ever change—they wouldn't dare! We had a hard time getting him to agree to stay at the Beverly Hills Hotel because he wanted to stop at his old haunt on Olvera Street. Olvera, way downtown, is the oldest street in Los Angeles.

The fact that Hollywood is the movie capital did not impress my father, as he was an infrequent movie-goer, and when dragged by my mother, he paid little attention to the screen. Mother, on the other hand, loved movies and, like most women of her day who went to beauty parlors, she read fan magazines from cover to cover. One night we all went to Chasen's Restaurant for dinner. It turned out to be the night of a big movie premiere, and most of the stars were present. Daisy was in seventh heaven, especially since a number of them stopped at our table to say hello. My father was oblivious to all this, as he was dividing his attention between some I. W. Harper and a busboy who, he discovered, came from Cleveland. My mother was so excited that at one point she poked my father in the ribs and said, "Russell, pay attention! Look! There's Greer Garson!"

"Oh," said Pop indifferently, "you mean that fellow who used to room with Jimmy in New York?" Of course, he was referring to Garson Kanin. (My father had a knack of getting people's names slightly confused and refused to stand corrected. He never even learned not to call Henny "Penny.")

We tried to show Russell and Daisy around, but Dad would have none of it. He said, "Look, son, whenever I'm looking at a project to buy, I always like to look it over by myself. I'm the kind of fellow who likes to study things alone. Without any outside pressure. Let your mother and me go from place to place, and I'll give you a fresh viewpoint of the entire situation."

What situation he had in mind, I'll never know. So, armed with passes, which, believe me, were even then not easy to get, Dad and my mother made a tour of all the studios. When they got back that night, he settled himself on the sofa, bourbon and pipe at hand, for a long chat.

"Now," he said, "here's a businessman's observation. You can take it for what it's worth. Here's the way I size up where you should work. The first place you sent me, Metro-Goldwyn-Mayer, is too decentralized. I don't care whether you're making bottle tops or pictures, the whole thing has got to be designed like an octopus—everything coming out from the center. When it comes to architecture, you can't beat old Mother Nature. Now the second one— I've got it right here—yes, it's called Twentieth Century-Fox. They've got too much land. They're land-poor. The taxes'll eat 'em up alive. Then, the other place we visited, Columbia, out of the question—too many wooden buildings. Looks like Asbury Park. It's a firetrap. Someday the whole thing'll go up in smoke. Son, I've got to go along with my original suggestion. Howard Hughes's operation, RKO. As we went in there, I saw a fellow painting the outside wall. And you bet your boots that attitude of improving the outside goes right through to the very core of the organization."

Well, my dear old dad wasn't too far wrong. Six months later Columbia Studios caught fire and darned near burned to the ground, and land-poor Twentieth Century-Fox turned their back lot into a subdivision, which is now Century City, no less!

One day I went to see my agent in Beverly Hills and Pop came along. I said, "Pop, I'm going to be about an hour. Do you want to come in with me, or would you rather wait in the car?"

"Don't worry about me," he said. "I'll just take a little walk."

When we met at the car, I asked my father what he had done.

He said, "Jim, I got a little thirsty and went and had a glass of beer. By accident, I stumbled on one of the prettiest bars I've ever run across. I'll bet you've never even been in there. It takes someone from out of town with a fresh viewpoint to find these out-of-the-way spots. The owner is a nice little fellow, too, and he's out to get business. He even chills the glass. Would you believe it, I was the only one in there. Why, the fellow must be starving to death. I told him, I said, 'I don't know how you ever expect to get anyone in here. You're on Rodeo Drive, that's just a little side street.* You don't even have a sign out front.' I said, 'Rip out all these empty tables, put in a bowling alley. Serve a dollar dinner. Lose money for a while, but get 'em in.' C'mon, son, I'll start the ball rolling for the guy and buy you a drink in there.''

The little out-of-the-way spot that Pop had discovered was Romanoff's Restaurant, at that time one of the most expensive and exclusive in the country and, along with Chasen's, one of the two most celebrated eating places in our town.

It may be a coincidence, or perhaps Romanoff took his advice, for just a few months after Pop's visit, it moved to a busier location. We are still waiting, however, for the dollar dinner.

One night we took Pop out on the town and wound up, just before closing time, at Pop's little hideaway, Romanoff's. We ran into that wonderful actor and charming man, Herbert Marshall, and his lovely wife, "Boots." Bart, as he was known to his friends, invited us back to his house for a nightcap. We had a delightful time, and Bart was wonderful to Dad. He told his fabulous stories of his experiences in the war, showed his letters from Winston Churchill, and brought out his great collection of original cartoons. After an hour or so, Boots left us and went to bed. I must admit we stayed on. Finally, as we were saying good night at the door, Pop said, "I had a great old

---

*Rodeo Drive: It may have been a little side street then, but may Cartier and Gucci have mercy on my soul!

time, Ronnie. Say good night to Bonita for me." Dear old Dad had scored again!

Henny and I have often wondered whether Dad said those things because he really didn't know, or because he was trying to pull our leg. We rather think that my father had hit on a comedy format and played it to the hilt.

I was aware very early in life that Pop wasn't like any of the other parents; neither was my mother, Daisy. Naturally I wanted them to be like all the other mothers and fathers, but they were so different. All kids are embarrassed by their parents at one time or another, but I never knew what to make of mine. They were totally unpredictable, which tended to keep me on my guard. I remember when I was fifteen and going to Kentucky Military Institute, they turned down the invitation to attend the Homecoming Weekend—then suddenly they simply showed up! I was thrilled, chagrined, confused, and elated, and, as usual, they charmed me. They informed me happily that they would attend every one of the functions!

I was proud and thrilled when Mother was chosen to review the battalion at a special dress parade. I remember "Eyes right" as we passed in review. I could clearly see beautiful Daisy, very military, chin up, at attention—but saluting the colors with the wrong hand over the wrong breast. My not-too-large circle of friends also were charmed by Mother and Pop, and Daisy was flattered no end when they asked for her scarf to be Company C's colors to fly from their guidon. Mother made a cute little speech in which she called the cadets in Company C her "special soldier boys." My mother lived in a Warner Brothers world. We didn't have the heart to tell her that "Flirtation Walk" was a hook shop at Second and Main.

One of the highlights of Homecoming was the football game between the KMI lightweight team, of which I was right tackle, and our traditional rivals, Saint Matthew's Junior High. Later, when we had amassed 138 points against our opponents' 0, they presented me with a little gold football that had the score engraved on it. I was so proud of that little charm. But during Homecoming, while our goal line remained unsullied, this was about to change, as the Saint Matthew's juggernaut roared down the field to our three-yard line. However, the day was saved! By *my* flying tackle, and the final gun, in that order.

Later that evening, when I presented myself at my parents' hotel for dinner, proudly sporting my gold football charm and a brave little bandage over my right eye, Pop and Daisy admitted they had left the game early for a very select mint julep party. They had missed seeing me save the day! I know it sounds silly, but it still hurts.

Pop was a fascinating fellow, bright, amusing, sometimes a pal. But as a father? Well, I guess he was a parent of his time, maybe his class—I don't really know. For example, why did they shunt me off to University School, which I attended after KMI? It was local, right in Cleveland, a country day school. So why did I have to board there and be away from them? I could have come home every night. As for KMI . . . well, military school was Mother's idea. It was a trend . . . all her friends . . . etc. "You'll wear such a cute little uniform," she told me. Besides, she couldn't hear me from her fluffy, perfumed cloud of luncheons, fittings, and parties. I only saw her when she came home to change. And as for Pop, I never really could get through to him. He didn't know I had one big problem that I had been trying desperately to discuss with him. He never suspected that I didn't want to go to college or go into business with him. I kept trying to tell him I wanted to be an actor, but he treated it as though it were some kind of childish whim. He blew me off with, "Fine! When you're with R. G. Backus and Company Enterprises, you can do all the acting you want in those shows at the Hermit Club." I tried everything to get his attention. Time and again I said, "Pop, you don't understand! I want to go to New York and be a *real* actor!" He would take a puff on his pipe, lean down to his dog, and say, "C'mon, Duke, it's time for our walk." He didn't even hear me!

And they were always off somewhere, Pop and Daisy, one trip or another. "Wa Wa," my grandmother who lived with us, raised us—my sister and me—with the help of Olive, who had been with us since I was a baby. Well, they gave me everything they thought a boy could want—electric trains, bicycles, a saxophone, a Brooks Brothers charge account, and later a car. . . . I guess we all know why.

In the Rough

Back home in Bratenahl, the Country Club golf course was one of the oldest in the United States. The bunkers were inverted *V*'s with sand on either side. There were four enormous potholes thirty to forty feet deep, and the more skilled golfer could save a shot by using a midiron and hitting over the main line of the New York Central, which ran right through the course. It may seem pretty Mickey Mouse, but in its day it was a fine test of golf. It was the kind of course where you could par one hole and then get caught in one of the bunkers on the next one and shoot a ninety. Some very famous golfers like Bobby Jones, Jug McSpaden, and Tommy Armour used to play there long before my time . . . and later a young upstart who had not yet turned pro named Arnold Palmer.

While attending Bratenahl School, when I was about nine years old, I was a busy little bastard—caddying, taking golf lessons, playing goalie in a pickup hockey team, and directing two plays at once, *Cinderella* and *The Sleeping Beauty*, which ran simultaneously. This wasn't easy, as both leading ladies, Betty Ann Burton and Martha Jane MacLaughlin, were in love with me. I found that out when I coached them privately in my tree house.

My big source of income at that time was caddying at the Country Club, or shagging balls for the pro, Joe Martin, when he was giving lessons. Joe's rate was seventy-five cents a lesson, minus the five cents he gave me. It was this great underpaid pro who gave me my golf lessons while sitting in an old deck chair wearing a worn, ill-fitting three-piece suit—a gift from a member—and taking frequent swigs from a bottle he had stashed under a bush. That's a far cry from the pros of today who fly corporate jets, who own and control several golf courses, and who make millions in endorsements. In those days pros were in the same category as caddies, and they were required to use the back door of the clubhouse. The first time this unwritten law was broken was after a heated round at Saint Andrews when David, the Prince of Wales, invited his partner, the great Walter Hagen, into the clubhouse to have a "Wee Doch 'n' Doris" with him.

Between sessions, Joe Martin taught me how to play "the old and ancient game." He explained the basic swing. He also taught me how to grip down on an old mashie (this was right before numbered clubs replaced names), how to punch a ball quail-high into the wind, and how to bump a shot into the long green. I remember a little bush about fifty yards from the practice tee. Joe would take a wary nip from his practice bottle, then toss out ten balls. "Hit the bush with eight of these," he'd say. "You're into the wind, Jimmy, so punch a mashie." I was a good pupil. I practiced or played every chance I got. I couldn't get enough of the ancient game.

Some forty years later I was Ken Venturi's partner in the L.A. Pro-Am. I had pushed my shot over the green and coming back had very little green to work with. Ken came toward me. "Let's look this little dude over," he advised, eyeing my ball. "Got any ideas?"

"Yes," I said. "I'm going to open the blade on this sand iron, open stance, break my wrists quickly, then on the way down I'll firm my wrists and hit down and through."

So I did just that and damned near holed the shot. Venturi walked over. "What the hell kind of a club is that? A wooden shaft?"

"It's a Joe Martin sandblaster," I told him.

"Well," kidded Ken, "don't try to cross the border with it—it's an illegal weapon!" Then he added, "I'd like to meet whoever taught you that one!"

At that moment I thought I heard a faint rumble of thunder in the sky.

This Is Henny . . .

Jim's father was a pretty good golfer. He could have been a fine one if he had practiced, but with his handicap he was darned near unbeatable. He told me that Jimmy used to caddy for him once in a while, carrying those clubs that were longer than he was. After the foursome was out on the course, Jim's father would say, "How about letting the little fellow play a few holes?" Then, sucking them in, he would add, "If we get in anyone's way, we'll just let them play through." They would laugh tolerantly and wave the kid on. Someone was sure to announce laughingly, "Bet you he misses." Pop would half-kiddingly take on the bet. Another would volunteer, "Let me in on this. He's sure to hit it on the toe." Then Pop, going along, would advise his son, "All right, my boy, take it easy. Keep your eye on the ball." By this time, Jim's father informed me, "That little devil had teed up the ball, then he gave it a slight forward press, brought it back low and slow, kept his little tousled head right over the ball, and followed through . . . and that ball rifled out a good two-hundred-and-fifty yards!" Of course, Pop never took their money. It wasn't much later that the ten-year-old Jimmy became a child golf champion playing charity matches with Walter Hagen.

This Is Jim . . .

Golf has been my passion ever since I was a child. Environment had a lot to do with it, I guess. At Madison we lived on a fairway, which made it handy. We've all seen pictures of the traditional American boy who is generally depicted as a barefoot boy with cheeks of tan. We, too, had cheeks of tan, but, instead of the fishing pole they invariably carried, we were packing a sack of cut-down golf sticks—each with a personality of its own.

In the movie *Pat and Mike*, I played a golf pro and Katharine Hepburn played a madcap heiress who is an amateur golf champion who goes on to win the Ladies Open. They signed the ranking lady golf champions to play themselves in the tournament scenes against Miss Hepburn. I remember such fine golfers as Helen Detweiler, Beverly Hansen, Helen Hick, and—the greatest lady golfer of them all—Babe Didrikson. We shot most of it at my home course, the Riviera Country Club, and the rest of it at the Ojai Valley Country Club, a delightful little spot near Santa Barbara. Hepburn had a fair country swing but got obstinate when Willie Hunter, the Riviera pro—and a fine one at that—tried to help her by changing a few things in her game so that it would look like she could conceivably beat those lady pros. She was just as stubborn about her wardrobe. That year the lady golfers were wearing short pull-over sweaters, cute little swing skirts (pants were frowned upon), fancy belts, and multicolored golf shoes. Miss Hepburn showed up in jodhpurs, a silk blouse, and jodhpur boots. She even insisted on wearing this outfit in the picture.

The character I played was that of a celebrated golf pro who spots her in a tournament and offers to take her on as his protégée. Miss Hepburn is a hell of an actress, and I loved working with her, but away from the camera she can be a real pain in the ass. She spent a lot of her time trying to impress the lady pros who, when not actually shooting, were out on the golf course chipping balls, putting for money, and talking about . . . what else? . . golf! What teed Hepburn off above all was the fact that Babe Didrikson was completely unimpressed by her. Hepburn did everything to get her attention. She had just finished doing *The African Queen* with Humphrey Bogart. One day when we were shooting out on the course, and a good half mile from the clubhouse, a mammoth Cadillac limousine came lumbering across the fairways—an attention getter if ever I saw one! And out of the limo in true Hollywood style stepped Humphrey Bogart himself! In person! Not a motion picture! Hoping to shake Miss Didrikson's tree, and with a triumphant gloat in her voice, Miss Hepburn shouted, "Look who's here! It's Bogie! . . . Bogie! . . . Bogie!" The Babe spun around. "Lady, never say that word on a golf course!"* she barked as she drilled a drive down the fairway 275 yards from Bogie! Bogie! Bogie!

The Babe and I had many rounds of golf together. She was the only golfer, male or female, who had complete control of the ball. It was magic! Particularly so when you realize that she played her last tournaments while suffering from cancer. In the years I played with her, she taught me shots I couldn't believe were real and didn't believe I could ever master. When she became very ill and was in great pain, her husband, George Zaharias, begged her to stop playing. In 1954, he pleaded with her to forgo the Open sponsored by the Ladies Professional Golf Association, which she had previously won in 1948 and 1950. "Just one more, George," she begged. She won it and checked right back into the hospital.

Babe had a salty sense of humor and loved jokes. In those days I used to replace Dave Garroway on the *Today* show

---

*Bogie: The second most horrendous word you can utter on a golf course, meaning, "One over par," a mediocre score for a pro. The worst word, however, is "shank," which is almost as bad as whistling in a dressing room.

for the month of August so he could have some time off. Knowing Babe watched the show every morning from her hospital bed, I would slant little gags in her direction. She loved it. I used to call her after the show. It was good to hear her laugh again. She was sick for a long time, but I never heard her complain. Never a "Why me?" What a champion she was!

Some time after Babe died, I played a round with her husband. After the game he asked me to walk with him to his car. He thanked me for all those stale jokes I told on the air, told me how it helped ease her pain. Then he opened the trunk of his car and pulled out a club. "Babe wanted you to have this," he said as he handed it to me. It was her famous wedge, the one she had used for more than fifteen years, that she had filed to a razor sharpness . . . the one with which she had won so many tournaments. I was speechless! And enormously touched. The Babe's wedge— I examined it with love. There were still drying tufts of grass on it and a tiny lump of sod—and a white mark from the ball she had pitched home in that last tournament. I thanked George and carefully carried it to my car and proudly put it beside me on the front seat. When I got home I put it on the mantel in the den with full intentions of taking it first thing in the morning to be mounted and entirely encased in glass to preserve the scratches, the grass, the sod, and the little white ball mark.

I awoke early, almost before Henny, and ran down to check on my precious club. It was there all right, resting in the same spot on the mantel, gleaming in the California sunshine. Gleaming? . . . Shiny? . . . Where were the tufts of grass? Where was the lump of sod? Where was the wonderful little white ball mark? I was about to turn on Henny when in through the doorway came Alice, our trusty maid, with a wide, self-satisfied grin. "Isn't it beautiful, Mr. Backus?" She beamed. "I cleaned and polished it real good!" As I was about to cry, she added, "Oh, by the way, a Mr. Shanks called."

This Is Henny . . .

As I sit here at the window seat in our bedroom, I can see Jimmy hitting plastic balls over the garden gate, over the pool, and sometimes over the house. I hold my breath with each lift of the club. He's better! He's doing better! This man who so loves to play what the golfers call "the ancient game" hasn't played a round in six years. For too long he couldn't stand up, let alone swing a club. Often I'd see him stealing sad little glances at his many trophies in the den. I moved a few of them a little while ago when I was doing my weekly polishing. The one he got in Texas for coming in second at the Houston Pro-Am. Beside it the photograph of himself and Trevino in the beautiful silver frame he was given after he had played a golf match with Lee on national television. And his favorite of all, the silver sculpture he received when he and Canadian pro George Knudson came in fourth at the prestigious Bing Crosby Tournament in Pebble Beach in 1964.

He's working every day now with that fine teaching pro, Walter Keller, determined to play once again in the Crosby. And he'll do it! He'll come back like the champion he is, and I'll tenderly place another prize I'll have to polish somewhere in that crowded room.

Go on, sweetheart. Belt it, champ! I know you can do it! And don't forget, the gazebo is a hazard!

The Old Vic

Three or four times a year my phone will ring, and when I answer it a voice barks, "Abbott, Alcott, Anderson, Backus, Banks, Barrett, Culpepper, Davis J., Davis L." By now I know it is the roll call of Company C from Kentucky Military Institute. The roll call continues: "Ettinger, Featherstone, Goodpasture, Huddleston." I know from experience that I have time to go to the kitchen and get a Diet Coke. I pick up the phone just as the call is winding down. "Vaughn, Wilson, Woodruff, Yancy, Yundt. COM-PAN-EEE! AT-TEN-SHUN! DISSS-MISSED!" I hear a click on the other end, so I hang up, too.

That was one of my dearest friends calling from his home in Rancho Santa Fe. This was his way of saying, "How have you been? . . . We miss you. . . . Everything is fine here. . . . We send our love." Explain it? I couldn't begin to. And, even though he is one of my oldest friends, it would be easier to explain Stonehenge than Victor Mature.

We first met at Kentucky Military Institute when we were of junior high school age. We were brought together by the common knowledge that we were not cut out for the military life and that we had to get out of there, but fast!

We were thrown together a lot in school because we repeatedly drew the same punishments. Our two most constant offenses were the unmilitary state of our rooms and our persons. We were each known as "Cadet Slob."

The boys who behaved and obeyed the rules were allowed to go into town every Monday. In the years Vic and I went to KMI, we never once made it! We made up for it, however, by giving jolly, illegal cocktail parties in our quarters. This being Prohibition, we served a delightful and very potent drink: lemon soda and Aqua Velva shaving lotion. Our bar was a hole under a loose board in the floor.

One day we were on the brink of expulsion and were called up before the Colonel. Vic, when cornered by the authorities, had a way of infuriating them even further by becoming excessively military. He would click his heels, salute every word, and agree with every charge hurled at him. When the Colonel threw a thunderbolt at him like, "You are the worst cadet in the hundred-year history of this academy," without taking a beat, Vic would click his heels, salute a shade too smartly, and answer, "Yes, sir!" (salute and click). "You're absolutely right, sir!" (more saluting and clicking). "I agree with you one hundred percent, sir!" (more of same). "I'm terribly sorry, sir!" (windmill of salutes and clicks).

By now the Colonel was enraged. "Cadet Mature," he shouted, "I'm never wrong about one of my cadets, and I predict you will wind up in the gutter, a bum! You're guilty of insubordination, your quarters are a disgrace, and you're constantly out of uniform! Why, you wouldn't last five minutes at the Point! With this disgraceful record, what actually are your plans when you get out of here?"

"Sir," said Mature eagerly, with great clicking and saluting, "I'm going out to Hollywood and become a movie star."

This was too much for the Colonel. Smoke came out of his ears as he yelled, "Get out! Be a movie star. Never heard of anything so ridiculous. I suppose you're going with him, Backus? Well, get out! Get out, both of you! And as long as you're in this academy, and I'm sure that won't be too long, stay out of my sight! Just stay out of my sight, both of you! Get OUT!"

Twenty years later, Vic and I were reunited for the first time. He hadn't changed a bit. He looked exactly the same as he had at fourteen. We were making a picture called *Interference* at RKO Studios, and we got to reminiscing about our days at dear old KMI. Suddenly Vic got an idea. The set we were working on was a beautiful Park Avenue penthouse. He called over two scantily clad starlets, got the prop man to give us four glasses and a magnum of champagne. We filled the glasses, put the starlets on our laps, and asked the still-man to shoot a picture of us. The picture turned out perfectly, and Vic sent it off to the Colonel with an appropriate autograph:

> Best wishes from Cadets Mature and Backus.
> P.S.: What are your honor students doing?

I remember on all three pictures I made with Vic, as soon as they called "Cut!" on the last scene of the day, he would streak off the set—shedding studio property as he went, leaving behind him a trail of makeup and wardrobe people gathering up his clothes, wig, beard, and shoes. It was required that everyone in the cast from the star on down leave everything that was worn on the picture with the production company for safekeeping. With Mature in the cast, they would order seven or eight doubles for every change he had, as things kept disappearing. And of course he would dump any suits, togas, armor—anything that was left over at the end of the movie—into the trunk of his car. I had a chance to check out his car trunk once. There were five suits, including tails and a suit of armor, two gallons of distilled water, a cigar box containing a long black wig, and a bridge lamp!

Vic was so used to costume pictures that he often forgot he was wearing strange wardrobe and sometimes even stranger makeup, the most hideous of which was in *Samson and Delilah*. It was for the gristmill scene where he had been tortured and his eyes put out. Thanks to the cosmetic wizardry of the makeup department, his eyes looked like two huge empty sockets. It was amazing. From a very short distance you couldn't see his eyes at all, just two black gaping holes. This very bizarre makeup didn't deter Vic from fleeing the set as soon as he was unchained so he could dash home and hit some golf balls before it got too dark. He would leap into his convertible with the top down and screech off. Can you imagine pulling up to a red light next to that?

This Is Henny . . .

Vic, like Madame Pompadour, conducted his business in the early morning hours from his dressing room. Quietly, and with very little fanfare, he had acquired a financial complex whose giant tentacles encompassed an entire city block. It included every kind of store imaginable, including the then ubiquitous Chinese laundry run by the owner in sateen slacks and a long queue, and a shoe repair shop with a cobbler named Tony who wore earrings and a bandanna. If nothing else, Vic cast—or rather rented—to type. But the jewel in his crown was "Victor Mature's Television Store"—the first in West Los Angeles, and where Jim and I got our first set. Talk about being the first boy on your block! This was in an area of newly married ex-G.I.s, who did nothing but watch early TV and make love. So naturally, business was booming in the TV store. His megalopolis also included a drive-in pediatrician, which was a great convenience to those young marrieds who were contributing so much to the Pico Boulevard baby boom. And, so they shouldn't waste too much time away from their TV sets, the pediatrician was right next door to "Victor Mature's Tropical Drive-in and Take-out" and the home of "Mature's Canned Meatballs."

This Is Jim . . .

Vic also used his dressing room as a display lounge for his endless cans of meatballs, which he and I consumed every day for lunch, and his TV sets with the prices carefully marked on little white cards which were pasted to their magnifying bubbles. The English actors at the studio were appalled that a big star like Mature was "in trade," but the sight of someone like Hedy Lamarr perched atop a Zenith was pretty strong stuff . . . especially at 6:45 A.M.

Early one morning Vic's business manager arrived to tell him that Internal Revenue was looking into his returns. They were particularly concerned with his entertainment expenses. "Don't worry," said Vic. "Have the man from the IRS come to lunch with me." Reluctantly, the business manager made a date for the IRS representative to meet Vic and his stand-in, secretary, and press representative for lunch at Lucy's the following day. I went along.

Lucy's was a restaurant directly across the street from the studio. The IRS man was the first to arrive. Vic was late and was the last to be seated. Since they were still shooting Samson chained to the gristmill, he naturally arrived in full makeup—complete with some additional welts, scars, and sores along with his two bloody holes for eyes. The IRS man found himself hard-pressed to talk to a pile of rags, not to mention two bloodshot holes, about things deductible. "Sorry," said Vic, "I only have half an hour for lunch. I never have time to change." The IRS man got the full message when Vic was presented with the giant bill for lunch, which he paid without batting a hole!

In 1951 Vic and I were in the movie version of Shaw's *Androcles and the Lion*. He played the Captain and I played the Centurion, which is the Roman version of a top sergeant. This was an especially tough picture because we were due in makeup every morning at six to have our hair curled. Also, it took us a full hour, and three wardrobe men, to get into the authentic Roman armor. Take my outfit, for instance. First I got into my part-the-feet-in-the-middle sandals, with their leather thongs that wrapped around the legs up to my knees. Then came a suede night-shirt, followed by a skirt made of long, heavy leather straps studded with chunks of iron, under which I wore flesh-colored panties, for obvious reasons. Over this went a chemise made of steel chains. This was gathered in by a giant belt from which hung two tremendous jeweled swords. There was a June Allyson collar made of chains and medals from which hung a fifteen-foot red plush "Loew's Pitkin" curtain. On both arms I wore classical butcher's cuffs of cowhide in which were stashed two daggers. To top all this off, there was a helmet with a crazy ponytail down the back. When they first put this helmet on me, it was so heavy I blacked out, so they had to line it with sponge rubber to prevent a concussion. For accessories, I had a gnarled club in my left hand and a spear in my right. Now mind you, I was only a sergeant, so you can imagine what they hung on Mr. Mature!

Because parts of our bodies were exposed, we had to be shaved and covered with body makeup, which was applied with an ice-cold sponge at seven A.M. This outfit was so cumbersome and heavy that I actually had to be helped down even a single step by two men. I learned by the second day that to think of going to the boys' room in this rig was sheer madness. I was grounded in that department till I was pushed and pulled back to my dressing room at the end of the day. How the Roman soldiers ever raped or pillaged in this outfit I'll never know! And as for winning any battles, the enemy must have known far in advance that they were being snuck up on, for dressed like this—in this airtight regalia—the Roman army must certainly have risked offending.

But a man can get used to anything, and since we were on this picture for three months, we even got used to those costumes. In fact, there were times when we forgot we had them on. One day at lunchtime Vic said, "Look, we have an hour. I have to go to downtown Los Angeles to sign a legal paper. The lawyer's secretary's going to be waiting in front of the building so I won't have to get out of the car. You wanna come along?" It being a warm day, I was glad to go and delighted to leave the musty studio and get a breath of fresh air.

We drove the fifteen miles to downtown Los Angeles, the secretary met us, Vic signed the paper, and we headed back for the studio. As we were driving through one of those depressing neighborhoods that every city has, we decided to stop and have a drink. We pulled up in front of a faceless cocktail bar with an original name like "Ace Café." We slapped on our helmets, grabbed our spears, and went in. Coming from the blazing sunlight into this dark cave, we were momentarily blinded. We finally made out a bar and one guy with an obvious hangover who was quietly nursing a beer. The bartender, who was busy polishing glasses, had his back to us. As we approached the bar, Vic said, "Two Scotch and sodas, please." When the bartender turned and saw two giant Roman soldiers standing there in the half-light, he was speechless, he was paralyzed; he just stood there, frozen. After waiting for half a minute while the bartender simply stared in utter terror, Vic said, "What's the matter, don't you serve members of the armed forces?"

During the shooting of *Androcles*, a rare thing happened. We got an afternoon off. Vic asked me what I was going to do.

"What am I going to do? I've got an afternoon off, so I'm going to play golf."

He said, "Play golf? Well, I must admit I've never played, but I've got a whole lot of clubs, a bag, and some balls in the back of the car. I just won them in a raffle."

I later found out the truth about the raffle. The husband of one of the extras on the picture had suddenly died, and to raise money she was raffling off his golf clubs. Vic bought all the chances and slipped her an extra hundred besides. So off we went to the links. It was the first time Vic had ever had a club in his hand, but it was love at first sight. And then and there the world's most ardent golfer was born.

Two days later Vic joined the club Henny and I belong to—Riviera, which has one of the finest courses in the country—and started one of the great sagas in golfing history. He would arrive at the club at six in the morning before the course was open. He solved this by getting a master key to the clubhouse and putting a caddy under personal contract. By eight A.M. he had loped around eighteen holes as an eye-opener. He would then join a foursome who were under the impression that they were getting an early start, and play another eighteen. Spying another group of cronies going off on the back nine, Vic would join them for nine holes before lunch. After lunch he would continue on, wearing out various foursomes, and play until after dark. He would then invite a gang back to his brand-new house on the edge of the course. After gobbling dinner, he would conduct his guests to the living room, where he had set up a miniature course. All hands putted until one or two in the morning. When he wasn't working on a picture, believe it or not, this went on every single day!

In his early golfing career Vic was always followed around the course by his faithful dog, Genius. I remember playing with Vic one day and, at the end of nine holes, he ordered Genius up the hill to the clubhouse. I asked him the reason for this, and he said, "Genius developed a wheeze, and his doctor says he can only play nine holes a day."

This Is Henny . . .

When Vic was making *Million Dollar Mermaid* with Esther Williams, which was the story of Annette Kellerman's life and set in 1908, they made him two identical pairs of high-button period shoes. When they make up an actor's wardrobe for a picture, they always duplicate each item in case of accident or loss. These shoes were made especially for him and were so comfortable he just loved them. He loved them almost as much as he loved to play golf. When the picture was finished, Vic took off with his beloved shoes. He ran straight for the golf shop, where he had spikes put in them. He is the only golfer in America who wears high-button golf shoes!

This Is Jim . . .

Mature has a native shrewdness that is refreshing and to some people very disarming. Once he was about to start a picture with a director, Henry Hathaway, who is a very dear friend of mine. In fact, Henry told me this story.

Henry was very charming socially, but when he started to work he turned into a monster. He ranted, raved, threw things, and had been known to reduce seasoned, hard-boiled actors to tears. Before the picture started, Henry invited Vic to his office. He was charm itself. He mixed a drink, settled down, and smilingly said, "Vic, I want to warn you, we're sitting here, getting along fine, and I like you. But once we start working I'm liable to call you a dirty bastard or even a lousy s.o.b., or I might even say you are a stinking dago. But remember, I don't mean it."

Vic thought for a minute, smiled, and replied, equally charmingly, "Sir, I want you to know something. When anyone calls me a dirty bastard or a lousy s.o.b., or even a stinking dago, I kick the shit out of him. But remember, I don't mean it either."

This stopped Henry in his tracks and he never raised his voice to Mr. Mature. One day, however, when rehearsing a scene, Vic forgot a line. In mute rage, Henry started kicking the chairs, slamming things, and darting fierce looks at Vic. Vic looked up at him and with childlike innocence said, "Uh-uh . . . pantomime counts, too!"

This Is Henny . . .

At one time, Vic was forced to go on location in darkest Africa. This was a move he fought, knowing full well that the script was a piece of crap that could more easily and cheaply be shot on the Twentieth Century-Fox back lot. He lost out to its very gung-ho director, whom he hated.

Once they had arrived in Africa and settled in their tents, the director took Vic down to the riverbank to show him where he would be shooting the first scene the following morning.

"Now, you, Vic, will be paddling up the river in a canoe when you . . ." That's as far as he got.

"No way!" said Vic.

"What do you mean, 'No way?' "

"I'm not going to do it. That river is probably full of crocodiles."

The white hunter, who was also technical adviser on the picture, stepped forward in all his glorious regalia—khaki shorts, wide-brimmed hat with the leopard-skin band and all. "Mr. Mature," he said deferentially, "believe me when I tell you you'll never see one. They have very sensitive ears. Can't stand a bit of noise. All you have to do is clap your hands and watch the creatures scurry away."

"No way!" repeated Vic.

"Tell you what I'm going to do, old chap. I'll stay up all night and every hour I shall fire my elephant gun. By morning I assure you there won't be a croc between here and Cairo."

"Uh-uh!" said Vic, as he turned on his heel.

"What do you mean, 'Uh-uh!' " screamed the director. "Why won't you do it? Give me one good reason!"

"Okay," Vic replied. "One of those sons-of-bitches might be deaf!"

One week later they were shooting that movie on the Twentieth Century-Fox back lot—where God intended them to be all along.

This Is Jim . . .

The last time I heard from Victor, he opened the phone call with the KMI motto, "Character makes a man!" Then he started shouting out the roll call, and, because it was my birthday, he threw in, "Peter Crazy Kelso! Tight Ass Good Pasture! And Do-Do Ripple." For a finish, he did his imitation of a bad p.a. system and cried, "Field Marshall Culpepper, your mother wants you!" and hung up.

Growing Pains

While I was attending KMI in the 1920s, my family and I spent our summers in Madison—Ohio, that is. These were among the happiest days of my life. We lived in a compound around the Madison Golf Lakeland Country Club, surrounded by fairly young marrieds with lots of children the same age as sister Katie and I. If you bought a lot and built yourself a house around the golf course, you were given lifetime membership in the country club. (Come to think of it, that's the way Bel Air started.) According to my father, this was the first time a real estate development of this kind was attempted. Pop, who was his own man, designed our house as a surprise for Mother, which, considering the fact that this was his first time out, wasn't too bad. It wasn't too orthodox, either, as he had managed to design on Lake Erie a country place that was a combination of New England saltbox and mountain hunting lodge.

He used to brag that he had incorporated the best features of both. This seemed to be okay with Mother, except when they got into one of their bickering arguments, which usually took place at our bar after "the sun went over the yardarm." Pop was generally able to terminate the discussion by assuring her that this little colony would soon be

alive with "the best people." The arguments stopped cold
one day when my delighted mother caught a glimpse of
Marnee Klump's children in a pony cart with a real English
nanny.

Madison Golf Lakeland was one of three separate town-
ships. There was Madison itself, complete with town square,
bandstand, Main Street, and drugstore. Oh, what a drugstore! It had those different-colored glass vials in the window, and when you went inside on a boiling day, it would
always be cool and semidark. And that intoxicating drugstore smell!

Then there was North Madison, which was simply four
corners with a gas pump on each and a real all-night eatery
down the street. Farther on, at the crossroads, there was a
country general store. Another two miles south and you
came to M. G. L. C. C. If you paused at the main gate, which
was on a knoll, you could see the new nine-hole golf course
they had added and the houses dotting the landscape, plus
the sprawling one-story clubhouse. And there in the far
distance . . . shimmering Lake Erie. Yes, Virginia, there was
a Lake Erie, and it did shimmer. Nowhere was there a piece
of our planet as lush, as warm, and as bountiful as that
part of Ohio. It was as if God had put the world on hold.

There were about seventy or eighty kids in our group
who were demographically the same. Our mothers and dads
were in their late thirties or early forties, though they seemed
ancient to us. Our meeting place was the club, where a
five-piece band played the tunes of the day. There was a
code of behavior, unwritten but inviolate. The girls, for the
most part, were leggy sun-bronzed colts who answered to
the names of Alice, Sally, Mary Jo, Betty, and Dorothy. The
Sharons and Marcys and Karens of the fifties, and Tiffanys
and Brittanys and Courtneys of today were yet to come.
All were from upper middle-class families who, by today's
terminology, I suppose could safely be tagged WASPs.

We kids were the torchbearers. We could do no wrong.
How could we? We were the biggest, the most powerful

nation in the world. "Don't mess around with the U.S.A."
We had whipped the Hun on his own turf. We had made
the world safe for Democracy. We had defanged the Kaiser,
booted his imperial ass into exile in Holland, where he was
chopping wood and writing to his *meshpucha* in England
congratulating them on one hell of a win. "Sorry," he wrote,
"we both couldn't have won. . . . Too bad what happened
to Nicky. Those Bolsheviks must mean business. But I
guess you just can't trust a nation where they dance sitting
down."

I spent most of my time playing golf and caddying. The
thirty-five cents a loop I got from the ladies at Bratenahl
Club was a thing of the past. Good players, low handi-
cappers want and need a good caddy and are willing to pay
for him. Also, most of them want a caddy to pack only for
them, a caddy who knows the breaks of the green, deceptive
distances, the best way to play certain holes, a shortcut on
the doglegs . . . and that can be learned only by playing a
course over and over and over again. Since there is always
a fair amount of money involved, they depend on the caddy,
and when they win, the caddy generally shares in their
good fortune. So a twenty-dollar tip was not unusual. Once
in a four-way match the guy I was packing won close to a
thousand bucks. He gave me fifty. He knew and I knew
that the breaks I gave him had meant the difference.

Most people don't realize how much money changes hands
in a golf match, and it's all done with cash to keep Uncle
Sam from becoming a partner. Almost every club has its
share of golf hustlers. In the Madison years it was almost
impossible to keep them out, but finally they would be
ousted. It's done the same way today. For example, Hubby
starts to come home two or three hundred dollars shy. The
little lady takes umbrage. So she calls her friends and hears
that their husbands are coming up light, too. They get
together and make a few calls to the Membership Committee. There is nothing more powerful than an enraged
women's auxiliary. Lysistrata should live so long! And

the hustlers move on. Since M. G. L. C. C. was a new club and located in the boondocks, it was an ideal nest for the hustlers and their pigeons.

How did they get in to play? Well, if you are from out of town, all you have to do is present your paid-up membership card from your home course to the starter. It helps, of course, to wrap a fifty-dollar bill around it. Our club was a cinch. Since it was part of a real estate venture, prospective buyers were more than welcome. Stalling on the buy was good for a week or two, anyway!

So to M. G. L. C. C. they came! The hustlers and their huge, custom-made registered golf bags with their names emblazoned on the side. These cyclopean reticules—with their extra pairs of shoes, boxes of high-test golf balls, a sweater or two, rain gear, three or four caps, some gloves, and a flask—were live-in golf bags to say the least. And heavy? I should know . . . I packed them! Carrying those bags all the way—eighteen long holes—and no carts back then.

The first time I saw Jerry he was getting out of a Chrysler 70 Roadster. Boy, was he ever smooth! I had been recommended to him by the starter and the caddy master. We teed off. My guy slammed that ball right down the middle, 265 yards. Notice how a caddy always says "we" when his player hits a good shot? Otherwise he is apt to say, "Get a load of the banana ball that guy just hit!" Jerry's partner that day was his pal, Carmen. They were head-to-head with Fred and S. G., two brand-new members. The eighteenth was a par-four, 385-yard hole with a hidden creek—a real fooler. By now there was five or six hundred dollars riding. Jerry reached for a driver. I grabbed his hand. "Sir," I said, "I know you can drive over that creek, but you'll wind up with a nasty downhill lie, so play short with your mashie now, then bust in with your midiron." We watched the two brand-new members tee off with their drivers. Jerry looked at me like I was crazy. "Sir, look, that's the way Leo Diegel and George Von Elm played it." "You caddied for those guys?" "No, sir, I played with them—charity match." "All right, kid, here goes," he warned me, "but I'd better make it or I'll break your knees with a midiron!" All I can tell you is, I left the course that night a hundred dollars richer! When he gave me that hundred, I thought to myself, That's pretty keen for just a walk in the park! Here I was, fifteen and a half, and the best darn caddy in the club—and what's more, I could cream a ball with the best of them! (So how come nowadays I can't even hit my hat?)

In the excitement we forgot that Jerry's car had a dead battery. I offered to drive him to wherever he was going, and where do you think that was? The Dells Club! I almost dropped dead. All the kids in our group were dying to go to the Dells Club. We talked about it all the time. There was gambling and booze, and we heard that they had very skimpily dressed waitresses—real showgirls—from New York! You had to have a lot of moxie* and pull to get in there. Then Jerry said that if I behaved myself he'd get me in for a drink. I could hardly wait! I could barely drive my beloved new convertible. Pop had given me his old Reo sedan, which I had painted bright red, and, with the aid of an acetylene torch, I had converted into a roadster. All the kids did that. No car has ever again meant that much to me.

Then, somehow, there we were—at the Dells! Jerry got out. I waited in the car while he had a whispered conversation with the guy on the door, who kept staring at me and my car and shaking his head "no." I don't know what Jerry said to him, but I saw him give the guard one of his "midiron to the knees" looks, and the next thing I knew I was inside! Inside the Dells—who would ever believe it?!

It was a never-to-be-forgotten night. I remember exactly how I felt. I can still see the beautiful Velita as she came sashaying over. My eyes were out on sticks! She was

---

*Moxie: A turn-of-the-century soft drink. Also, goy for "chutzpah."

wearing nothing but high heels and a little G-string like the girls in *Captain Billy's Whiz Bang*.* I knew she was a waitress because she was carrying a tray. And . . . she was wearing just a string for a brassiere! I could hardly look! It was full of money! That's where you were supposed to put your tips!

Jerry ordered an I. W. Harper and soda while I overwhelmed them by ordering a Ramos Fizz. But I really scored when I whipped out my hundred dollars and cried, "Drinks for everybody!" I felt just like Ricardo Cortez. When Velita came back with the drinks, I paid her, and when she brought me the change, she handed it to me and leaned over so I could tip her. I put a crisp new twenty-dollar bill in there, and she grabbed my hand and held it to her bosom. Then she leaned in farther . . . and then . . . she kissed me! And love came to Andy Hardy! I don't remember when Jerry took off. I don't remember how many Ramos Fizzes I had. All I know is that I was in heaven. A fuzzy heaven, to be sure.

Then I recall doing some of my impersonations for her. I charmed her with my Eddie Cantor, singing "Ida, Sweet as Apple Cider" in her little pink ear. She loved it. She suggested that I get up on the floor and do my stuff. Why not? I got up every Saturday night at our club dance. But this was the big time! I still remember how I regaled them with my Ed Wynn† to great applause. Then I rolled up a menu like a megaphone and sang "My Time Is Your Time" like Rudy Vallee. Suddenly everything began to look upside down, and the last thing I recall is Velita kissing me and walking me through the club and out.

Captain Billy's Whiz Bang: Captain Billy was an antediluvian Hugh Hefner whose racy magazine was very popular with the free lunch and sleeve garter set.

†With thanks to Ed Wynn: "A mugwump is a bird who sits on a fence with his mug on one side and his wump on the other." Actually a then-timely political reference!

I woke up slowly. My head was a hot balloon. This waking up had to be handled with care. I couldn't shut out the sound of the cows mooing and their little offbeat bells. The eyes! Open the eyes! It was hard to do. I tried to focus. "Don't panic!" I said aloud. "It's only a hangover." And then it all came back. She wouldn't let me drive, and I remember this motel bedroom and Velita undressing me —both of us overcome with laughter. How beautiful she was. . . . Not like those girls I had known all my life. . . . They all looked like my sister. Velita was different. No wonder I loved her. And I was sure that she loved me because—I gasped!—we did it! That's why! I did it! I felt a rush of ecstasy. I really did it! . . . Wait till I tell the fellas. "Oh, Velita," I whispered. "I love you!" Where was she, anyway? I looked around frantically. I'll write her a note. I rummaged through my pockets for my pen . . . WHERE WAS IT? AND WHERE WAS MY MONEY? Wait a minute, did I spend the whole hundred? MY FOOTBALL? My little gold KMI football, my lucky charm! And my watch?! What time is it, anyway? Oh, well, it doesn't matter. I'm in love, and I DID IT, so who cares? Suddenly my heart leaped. What am I saying?! I've been gone all night! Oh, my God, MY MOTHER'S GONNA KILL ME!

This Is Henny . . .

Years later, in 1953 to be exact, Jimmy and I had the pleasure of playing *The Man Who Came to Dinner* at the Rabbit Run Playhouse, in Madison—Ohio, that is—following Hume Cronyn and Jessica Tandy's very successful tryout at that beautiful summer theater in *Fourposter*. On our closing night, as I was walking through the meadow to our dressing tent in the semidarkness, a giggling gaggle of women caught up with me and asked for pictures. I handed out some pre-autographed photos in the moonlight and, as I turned to go, one of the ladies slipped something into my hand. When I reached the lamp-lit tent, I opened my fist and, sitting on my palm, was a tiny golden football. Clearly etched on it were the letters:

J. G. B.

KMI	– 138
OPPOSITION	– 0

Prep School

University School, located on the outskirts of Cleveland, was the next pit stop in my quest for an education. This prep school was a far cry from KMI. A combination of old school tie, pukka sahib, and Ohio raj, it was modeled after the English public school. The grades were called "forms" and the teachers were labeled "masters." It prepared you for entrance exams to Yale, Princeton, and Harvard, as those were the only colleges they recognized. We dressed for dinner. The wife of one of the masters was a hostess at each table, and manners were very important. We were very polite at University School. We called everyone "Sir," including the head master's dog.

After dinner we studied in our room until "lights out." There were no bed checks like those at KMI, where every three hours you were awakened by a blinding flashlight to make sure it was you in there and not an effigy! With no bed checks, I was able to climb out of the window at nine-thirty —all I had to worry about was getting back in before breakfast. Fortunately, my roommate had a car. My roommate was a wealthy young rounder who had a Chrysler touring car with tires mounted on the running board and a second windshield for the back seat. It was stashed in a nearby gas station.

There were two other schools in the area—girls' schools
—Hathaway Brown and Laurel, with a pool of young ladies
willing to climb out of their windows to join us for an
evening at the Patent Leather Club, where we drank silver
fizzes and danced—clutching, nuzzling, and rubbing—to
"Lullaby of the Leaves," "I Surrender, Dear," and "These
Foolish Things Remind Me of You." Then, sexually aroused,
we took our subdeb dates back to their respective seats of
learning—French kissing all the way. "Going all the way,"
however, was taboo, so I paced in my room till dawn with
a condition known as "hot rocks."

The school believed in that famous quote, "The battles
of life are won on the playing fields of Eton." So we had
obligatory field or gym. In the fall, you had your choice of
football, soccer, or tennis. In the winter basketball, swim-
ming, or wrestling, and in the spring track, baseball, or
golf. I remember for my winter sport I opted for wrestling
—a strange choice, but then why not? I had finally chosen
my calling—not pro golf but the theatre—and as an incip-
ient actor I thought of the show business angle. I thought
that all wrestlers were really actors, like the one who called
himself Fu Manchu, with the long silk robe and endless
moustache. Or the one known as Eric the Red, with those
horns. Or how about The Hillbilly, who entered the ring
carrying a rifle in one hand and leading a hound dog on a
rope with the other?

I spent a lot of time working on my "character" when
I should have been studying. Oh, it was going to be a
ball! Wrong! Greco-Roman wrestling is a far cry from Fu
Manchu, Eric the Red, or that Hillbilly with the dog. It's
a highly stylized sport, a physical-intellectual exercise,
exciting only to those who really understand it. Actually,
it's chess with muscles. The matches last forever. One
single hold can go for twenty minutes. It's not unusual for
the participants to doze off every once in a while.

We worked on mats in a monastic room that was redolent of liniment, wood alcohol, and sweat. We wore

brown leotards and a jersey, and I regretted my choice of this sport from the very first hold.

Every afternoon from three to six o'clock Mr. Wagner, our coach—a fiery little martinet who doubled as professor of French II—took over. He couldn't understand my not liking this drab sport and went out of his way to acquaint me with its glories by using me to demonstrate all the holds. This meant that I spent one or two hours every day in the embrace of this pompous idiot. To make it even more unbearable, he bragged that he had worn the same leotard for the past twenty-five years—a piece of information I had guessed from scratch.

One afternoon I was suffering from a major retroactive post-Christmas hangover when, as luck would have it, Mr. Wagner chose this day to demonstrate some new holds with me. I spent what seemed like years being thrown around the room and repeatedly pinned to the mat. I was holding on by my teeth. Pausing for a moment, he addressed the team. "I will now demonstrate my own special hold. I call it the Flying-Lock-Scissors-Crotch hold." With that, he leaped up and caught my head right between his legs, and with his crotch he ground me into the mat, his twenty-five-year-old leotard completely engulfing me! I flexed about like a gaffed trout, but to no avail. I tried every Greco-Roman hold in the book. I was desperate! The more I struggled, the more pressure he applied. Then something snapped in my head. Greco-Roman my ass! It came back with a rush . . . I had been taught dirty fighting at KMI by an old marine drill instructor, and I used it! I shot out of Mr. Wagner's crotch like a clay pigeon from a trap. I am the first—and perhaps the only—student ever to be expelled from any school for biting the master in the balls!

And that was the high point of my career at University School.

The Bombshell

The sun had gone over the yardarm at last, and the Backus clan had gathered in the den of our Bratenahl home. It was a nightly occurrence, but not always with the full cast. This night was different, and I'll certainly never forget it. We were all there—Pop; Daisy; my sister Katie; Wa Wa, a delegate without portfolio; me, heir, at that time, not too apparent; our longtime maid, that great non-abstainer, Olive; and Duke, a dog, pro tem.

Pop always had a resident dog who had the same rank and privileges as I did. Pop's dogs were very serene, with great presence and latent nobility. But when I was little, somewhere along the line we inherited a dog named, aptly enough, Skippy. Skippy was a frenetic canine, a wiry little mountebank who knew every trick of the trade; he was a born hustler. Tradition also had it that Pop was never dogless. When one of his dogs went to that great fire hydrant in the sky, he had another one warming up in the bullpen. Pop abhored all of Skippy's doggy tricks—walking on hind legs, playing dead, begging, bringing back the ball, and making love to your trouser leg. These were all in Skippy's repertoire. I felt responsible inasmuch as I had picked Skippy up at the dog pound, where he had not dis-

43

played anything but a quiet charm. He waited till we got home before he went into his act. Later we found out that Skippy was dumb beyond belief. Want to know how he left us? He jumped through the rear window of a car bound for California. Maybe he wasn't so dumb. . . .

The family used Skippy as a standard. In fact, they used us both. (It seems that at the age of four I knew a few tricks, too.) For example, when they saw a terrible movie, they'd say, "Skippy or Jimmy could have written a better one." Or a concert, "Skippy or Jimmy could have sung better." Or, mentioning no names, "Skippy or Jimmy would have made a better President." And so on.

Mother had her own dog, Mr. Chin—a Pekingese. No one could put a finger (you didn't dare) on where Mr. Chin came from. Out of a giant fortune cookie? All we knew was that he was glued to Mother. Mr. Chin was with us for fifteen years, and all during that time, not once did anyone except Mother dare to pat him or, for that matter, even make a move in his direction. From this little venomous fur ball came a hissing of jealous hate worthy of a king cobra. Early on, Mr. Chin had staked out his turf— Mother's lap—and his favorite time of day was the cocktail hour. He had a penchant for hors d'oeuvres made with seafood, particularly lobster, shrimp, and caviar, and woe betide anyone who went for any of the above. They would be greeted by the kind of demoniacal sounds that would turn Albert Payson Terhune* into Jack the Ripper. We finally gave Mr. Chin his own plate.

I remember when Mother, Kate, and I were posing for the *Cleveland Plaindealer*—some charity event or other. Mother was sitting regally beside Katie and me. After the photographer had spent a good hour posing us and lighting us with loving concern, just as everything was set, just as

---

*Albert Payson Terhune: Famous nineteenth-century artist best remembered for his painting *"The Stag at Eve"*—standard equipment for any Third Avenue saloon.

he was about to shoot the picture, he noticed Mr. Chin for the first time. "Is that a dog in your lap?" "What dog?" queried Mother innocently, as though her Peke were part of her wardrobe. Need I say that Mr. Chin was in that photograph?

Some fifteen years later, our family scattered to the four winds. No one knew what happened to Mr. Chin. He simply disappeared. We tried in vain to find him for Mother's sake. All we know is he left us. We didn't leave him.

Now I'm going to tell you about *my* dog, Chum. Chum was an English terrier. No one ever loved a dog as I did that sweet and most gentle of all dogs. Chum was above tricks—too much of a gent. He had the greatest sense of timing, worthy of a Barrymore. Believe it or not, when we first got Chum, I used to ride him like a pony, and he never made a bad move. Chum had class.

Then one day Chum fell ill with a fatal canine disease. I remember I made a warm bed for him next to the furnace. Part of his treatment was to keep him warm and to give him an eyedropper of cod liver oil every half hour. I knew it tasted terrible, so I did the time-honored procedure of holding his jaws together with my hands. I did it just once, and Chum looked up at me as if to say, "You don't have to do that to me." I didn't! I was giving him his 3:00 A.M. medicine when I felt a pat on my shoulder. I looked up. It was Pop. "You get some sleep. I'll take over till morning." It was one of those times when I felt close to Pop. We buried Chum in the backyard. Kate read the Twenty-third Psalm.

So on that memorable evening I was thinking of Chum as I watched my father alternate sips of his bourbon with loving pats to Duke. He put his arm around his beloved retriever, took another sip of his drink, and then he dropped the bombshell.

"I want you all to know that I've given this a lot of thought and, after weighing all the pros and cons, I have decided to allow Jimmy to go to New York to be an actor.

But first he has to learn how. I've investigated all the drama schools, and the best place of all is the American Academy of Dramatic Arts. So that's where he's going!"

This was indeed a bombshell! He had been dead set against it, but I had not passed the entrance exams to any of the colleges of his choice (probably a good idea on my part). And, even though Mother had said repeatedly that she wouldn't mind another Conrad Nagel in the family, he had been adamant. So what changed all this? Pop was really a very fair man, and after a long, sober, serious talk with me, he realized that I should be given this chance.

And what's more, Duke concurred!

Uncle Len

And so it was arranged. I was to go to New York to be an actor. Pop paid my expenses and my tuition in the American Academy of Dramatic Arts. But I was not to go unescorted. My social-climbing mother had managed to get an invitation from my uncle by marriage—my sister Kate's husband's uncle, actually, Len Hanna, who was going back to his New York home—for me to share his drawing room. Len was only too delighted to have company.

The East Cleveland station of the New York Central Railroad was always jammed at the end of the Christmas holidays with the boarding school set returning to their prep schools, finishing schools, and colleges. The boys were all wearing the uniform of the day—gray flannel trousers, blue Brooks Brothers button-down shirts with black knit ties, brown wing-tip shoes, polo coats with brown leather buttons, pigskin gloves, and snap-brim hats. The girls wore their version—twin cashmere sweaters (a pull-over and a matching cardigan), always, of course, with a string of graduated pearls, plus short skirts, polo coats with alligator buttons, scarves tucked inside, wool gloves to match, and broad-brimmed felt hats sporting long, jaunty feathers.

Surrounding the flower of Cleveland's youth was a ring of parental faces glowing with pride, tinged with bittersweet at the leave-taking. It seemed like only yesterday that they had been saying good-bye to their parents. Come to think of it, the names were the same—only the Roman numerals had changed.

There was a lot of good-natured shouting back and forth, like . . .

"Hey, Binky, going back to Groton?"

"Yeah, Mark, didn't see you at the club on New Year's Eve!"

"Hi, Muffy! I looked for you at the Wylies' last night!" This from Hunter Feibach III, known, naturally, as "Trip" for triple.

They belonged to the same clubs and went to the same schools. They grew up together as their parents had before them. They had their first fumbling sexual encounters with each other, and their fertility taboos and rites were as rigid in an unstructured way as those of the Hindu culture. They were literally thrown together like puppies and had their first "I'll-show-you-mine-if-you-show-me-yours" experiences as they played together on rainy days in a cluttered attic or in a musty old carriage house. Their first actual awakening occurred while dancing at the Wade Park Manor with subdebs like Phoebe Lambert or Sarah Houston, their white-gloved hands held high on the young lady's back under the watchful eye of Miss Flynn. Eventually they would marry one another.

This railroad station was their private preserve. It would never occur to any of them to go downtown. This suburban depot was convenient to their homes in Shaker Heights, Chagrin Falls, or Pepper Pike. The same stationmaster had always put them on the trains, and the smiling redcaps knew them and their luggage.

Once inside the station, which was still adorned in all its fading Christmas glory, Pop, Daisy, and I were heartily greeted by kids and parents alike. Kate had gone on ahead

to New York to find us a place to live. They were sending
her to take care of me and to help her recover from the
ordeal of her divorce from Mark Hanna, Uncle Len's *real*
nephew. We were all caught up in the usual bustling of
redcaps and luggage, checking of tickets, hugging, kissing,
and general mass confusion. Finally we untangled ourselves and made our way to the station bar.

It was packed. Pop somehow managed to push his way
through. The drinks he ordered were passed to him over
the customers' heads. There was a lot of shoving and a
great deal of noise. Everyone was hurrying. There wasn't
much time left. As Pop jostled his way from the bar to our
table, the orders were still being shouted to the bartender.
The kids drank Scotch. Their parents drank martinis, and
everybody smoked. The air was heavy with it.

A family friend stopped for a moment to wish us all a
happy new year. "Thank you, Fred," said Pop. "Daisy and
I hope to get to Lauderdale in February if that damn fool
in the White House doesn't get us into a war!"

We saw through the window a huge Lincoln limousine
as it barreled to a stop in front of the railroad station.
A chauffeur in formal livery leaped out and opened the
trunk. Jesse, everyone's favorite redcap, and his slightly
bent attendant, Truman, started to unload matching pigskin valises, overcoats on hangers, an attaché case, and a
gentleman's jewel case. The chauffeur opened the rear
door, and out stepped a middle-aged man carrying a Skye
Terrier, which he handed to his driver. He was an im-
posing figure—slightly bald, impeccably dressed in a sable-
collared overcoat. He looked about with sharp, imperious
eyes, which lit on the stationmaster. We watched him shout
to the stationmaster, who bowed and scraped Uncle Len
to the bar. Tommy, the bartender, had also seen Uncle
Len in the distance and had his drink already mixed and
waiting. He handed it to him as he passed.

Uncle Len spotted us at our table and joined us. He and
Pop started talking about me.

"I'm afraid he isn't going back to college," Pop said. "He wants to be an actor. I'm going to finance him for a year."

"Well, I think that's just fine," said Uncle Len. "It's about time we got some glamour in the family!"

"What?" asked Pop incredulously. "What did you say?"

"I mean it!" laughed Len. "I'm a frustrated ham myself. Can't act a damn. So . . . I do the next best thing. I quietly back plays. Had three hits last year."

Pop was astonished. "You hear that, Daisy? All Jimmy needs is a push in the right direction."

"I think I can make sure he meets all the best producers and directors on Broadway."

My heart thumped wildly. Pop just had time to thank Len for taking care of me before we heard, booming over the loudspeaker:

"THE *TWENTIETH CENTURY LIMITED* IS ARRIVING ON TRACK THREE! ALL ABOOOARD!"

Uncle Len and I climbed the little portable stair. We were helped by an impeccable, white-coated, smiling porter. "Welcome," he said, "to the *Twentieth Century Limited*."

The train started to move stealthily out of the station. I must say I felt a twinge in my heart. I looked out of the window and, following us as we pulled out of the station, were a converted Pop making encouraging gestures, followed by Wa Wa throwing kisses at the wrong train, and Daisy holding up Mr. Chin for a farewell snarl.

I made my way down the length of the car. I had stayed in the vestibule waving to my family until I lost sight of them. Uncle Len had gone on ahead to the drawing room to, as he laughingly put it, "set up housekeeping." The rocking motion of the train under way felt good.

The entire car consisted of upper and lower berths. At the end of each car was a drawing room with its lavatory, and opposite that a gentlemen's or a ladies' room. This was where the "uppers" and "lowers" performed their ablutions and dressed.

As I made my way up the aisle, I noticed the smoke and

the noise. From the closed curtains I heard talking and giggling and a muffled portable Victrola playing "Night and Day" with Fred Astaire on the vocal, which became that year's big hit song. I could hear the sloshing of liquor being poured into paper Dixie cups. I smiled tolerantly and thought, There but for the grace of God—and good old Uncle Len—go I!

Things were different in the drawing room. There was a sofa, two club chairs, two large windows, and some tables, one of which was covered with a snowy linen cloth, upon which sat a bottle of Scotch, some soda, and an ice bucket. A porter had just finished making up the upper and lower berths and was giving the pillows a final fluff.

Uncle Len freshened our drinks heavily, then raised his glass. "Well, best of luck, Jim. You're going to need it." We clinked glasses. Then he shot me a querulous look. "How did you ever get your dad to give in?"

"Well, it wasn't easy. You see, Dad believes in all those clichés. 'Actors are bums!'—'Shouldn't be allowed to vote!'—the works! But one thing about Dad, he's fair. Once he realized I meant it, we shook hands and that was that."

"What about your mother?"

"Oh, you know Daisy. She already has me living in sin with Helen Hayes! I want to thank you, Uncle Len. You've already helped," I said, becoming serious. "And letting me bunk in here, and—"

"You really think you have talent?" Len interrupted, mixing us another drink.

"Thanks," I said, accepting it. "Yes, I really do. But I know having talent doesn't do you much good unless you get a chance to prove it."

"That's where I come in. I'm what is known as an 'angel.' Everybody sends me scripts for backing money. I read them all. If I see a part you're right for, all I have to do is call the producer." Uncle Len's face lit up. "Listen, I'll arrange a little cocktail party to introduce my nephew.

You're the right sort. Good school, good family, father with money enough. The theatre is a whore. Respects only two things—money and success. You've got to get there the best way you can. Unfair, but true."

"You must know!" I said, glancing at my watch. "Gee, I'd better be turning in." I rose.

"Wait a minute." Uncle Len reached for the hook overhead where his jacket hung and took a platinum card case from the pocket. He extracted a card and handed it to me. "Here is my phone number and address. Let's keep in touch. Don't lose the card. I'm unlisted."

"Don't worry. I won't. And again, thanks."

I'll never forget that moment. I gulped the tag end of my drink, went to the ladder, and started to climb to my bunk. My feet barely touched the rungs. I crawled in and closed the curtains. What a swell guy Len is, I thought. I was deliriously happy. I remember leaning back on the pillow. I left the blue night-light on, lit a cigarette, which glowed in the semidarkness, and listened to the *clackety-clack* of the train as it swayed from side to side. God, those trains were wonderful way back in 1934. Now I could allow myself to dream a little of the wonderful things poised, ready to happen.

In the lower berth Uncle Len had his reading lamp on. He was nursing his drink. "Listen!" he suddenly called up to me. "I was just wondering about an agent for you. Oh, what the hell. Come on down and let's have a nightcap!"

"An agent!" I yelled. "Oh, boy!"

Ignoring the ladder, I actually leaped to the floor of the car.

"Mix us each another double. Make mine straight," said Uncle Len, "and come over here and talk."

I mixed the drinks. My hands were shaking. What a great guy, I remember thinking. Uncle Len accepted his drink and patted the blanket beside him.

"Sit over here and make yourself comfortable." He handed

me a pillow, and I arranged myself on top of the blanket with my uncle. We each took a big swig of our Scotch.

"Now," Uncle Len continued, "the first thing to do is get you an agent. The best one! Let's see—Leland. Yes, Leland Hayward. He's the one! I know! We'll have lunch! Organize the troops!"

As if drawn by some outside force, he suddenly, deftly, slipped his hand inside my pajama fly! I leaped out of the berth in utter shock. I did all but fly up the ladder to my upper. I stared straight ahead in disbelief. What was that all about? Could this really have happened to me? It was just not possible! I felt humiliated, confused, and degraded, and the tears actually jetted from my eyes. Uncle Len? It was just not possible!

The *Twentieth Century Limited* roared through the night.

The next morning I waited, trying to avoid seeing him. All he said to me in parting was, "Well, I guess it got a little damp out last night."

And I remember I said, the best way I could, "Thank you very much. Thank you for the drinks, the advice . . . the whole thing. It was a royal send-off."

"That's what uncles are for," said Uncle Len, hitting the word "uncle."

And that was the end of that!

The Academy

The American Academy of Dramatic Arts was, and still is, the most prestigious drama school in the country. It was the spawning ground of such diverse names as Cecil B. DeMille, Grace Kelly, Spencer Tracy, Jason Robards, Fredric March, Lauren Bacall, Robert Redford, Pat O'Brien, Hume Cronyn, Anne Bancroft, Edward G. Robinson, Ruth Gordon, William Powell, and, believe it or not, Don Rickles.

At that time, all I knew about the Academy was that it was in New York. I had been to that great city nine or ten times on carefully sanitized trips. I saw the Woolworth Building, the Aquarium, the Metropolitan Museum of Art, the Staten Island ferry, and of course, Coney Island—the Disneyland of its day.

My most vivid recollections of New York were culled from those vintage Warner Brothers sagas in which hundreds of girls played white violins and then tapped their way through Times Square. I knew that "Manhattan Babies Don't Sleep Late—It's Early in the Morning!" I found out early on that there was, in fact, "Love for Sale," but as Lord Chesterfield said, the price was exorbitant, the position ridiculous, and the sensation fleeting. And "The Bronx is up and the Battery's down; they go to work in a hole in

the ground!" I was under the impression that men wore
top hats and tails nightly and that invariably they would
hijack milk wagons driven by Allen Jenkins with Ruby
Keeler riding shotgun to get them home.

I knew that the American Academy of Dramatic Arts
was on Fifty-seventh Street, which I was certain was pretty
far uptown, because in one of those nocturnal emission
pictures Guy Kibbee and Dick Powell had a fight over Joan
Blondell on a subway platform which was clearly marked
"59th Street," and with one gliss of a harp later they were
in a cornfield dancing with Ray Bolger.

I didn't expect a football stadium at the A. A. D. A. Or
even a team. Or even "The Old Ox Road." But I wasn't
ready for what I got. My new school was loosely located
in the Carnegie Hall building which, even in those days,
was still erect, thanks to millions of termites holding hands
together in a suicide pact. It was so old and decrepit that
people thought I had dandruff—but it was only falling plaster. It's all right for a building to be old, but Carnegie Hall,
even then, abused the privilege.

It was the day of my interview at the Academy. What
did they want, I wondered as I walked along the avenue.
Ah, Carnegie Hall. . . . It was in all its ancient glory, right
where they said it would be, on the corner of Fifty-seventh
and Seventh. I tipped my hat to it for luck and made my
way in. There was a directory in the lobby with room
numbers for the A. A. D. A. all over it at random, inter-
spersed with studios and apartment numbers. I studied it
for a moment. . . . Fencing studio, Room 4A . . . Dance
studio, 6C . . . etc. I was looking for the office. There it
was, on the top floor. I got into the little wrought-iron
elevator and pushed the button. It went up and finally
stopped. The door opened on the fifth floor. I got out and
there was a maze of hallways that would confuse even Pepe
La Moko! Finally I saw a sign that read, "Use Alternate
Elevator for A. A. D. A. Office." I got into an even smaller
car and again I pushed the button, and again it rattled its

way up and stopped, and again the door opened and I got
out. And there was another sign, with an arrow that told
me to use the stairs. Half a floor down, in an annex of some
sort, there it was! At long last—the office!

Five minutes later I was chatting with a delightful man,
Mr. Emile Diestal. Mr. Diestal was dressed in a dark suit,
a vest with white piping, and a shirt with a wing collar.
He looked like he was on his way to finance the Suez Canal.
He handed me a marked script of *Lady Windermere's Fan*.
I bristled. I had already been accepted when Pop sent in
the check. So what was this—an audition? Mr. Diestal
smiled. "I just want to get your energy level and your voice
volume and tone." I read three or four lines, and he stopped
me. "You come over very well," he said, putting out his
hand. And then he said those magic words, "Welcome to
the A. A. D. A."

On the main floor was a locker room separated into two
parts, "boys" and "girls." It was presided over by Mother
Lingo, a tiny little old lady with a luminous quality. I
knew I had seen her someplace, and I had—in the theatre.
Like everyone else who worked at the Academy, she had
been an actress. We were each given a locker. We had no
showers, no sinks, no water in our rather pathetic dressing
room—just lockers that finally were filled to capacity
with our books, clothes, sneakers, ballet shoes, makeup
kit, and assorted treasures. This was where we met every
morning and where our assignments were listed on the
bulletin board. A normal class would have about fifteen
students, but sometimes, due to rehearsals or special classes,
there would be as few as three eager thespians in attend-
ance. A typical day for me was:

8:30 A.M.	Assembly Room with Mother Lingo
9:00 A.M.	Voice
10:00 A.M.	Library study
11:00 A.M.	Diction
Noon	Lunch

1:00 P.M.   Dancing
2:00 P.M.   Fencing
3:00 P.M.   History of Theatre
4:00 P.M.   Rehearsal

My schedule would vary from day to day.

The two-year course was divided into the Junior and Senior classes. The Junior class, aside from being taught the rudiments of acting, was one long audition—learning scenes for one part or another. There were about one-hundred-and-twenty students in the Junior class, ninety of them girls. Oh, boy, I remember thinking, smorgasbord! Most of the girls, once they found out what you had to go through to become an actress, bombed out or quit. What few boys there were at the Academy were, for the most part, on scholarships and were more motivated than the girls. At that time, acting was not the most popular profession for men. With this premium on male thespians, going from Junior to Senior class was a certainty for me, even though only thirty Juniors were asked back. Out of our entire class, only about four people made it, and only five or six more even stayed in the business. . . . Which gives you some idea of the rigors of the acting profession.

The thirty-member Senior class was in essence a stock company. We were cast in plays that had a three-week rehearsal period and played for one thrilling performance on Broadway with an invited audience composed of agents, talent scouts, patrons of the arts, and fellow actors. We did one of these every month at the Belasco Theatre, usually a matinee, given on an off afternoon when the theater was dark.

The teachers, who doubled as directors, were all working actors and were not above moonlighting between engagements to keep their creative juices flowing. Among the teachers in my time were Joseph Schildkraut, Margelo Gilmore, Emlyn Williams, and a little later, Rosalind Russell and Kirk Douglas.

To the right of the lobby in the Carnegie Annex was an

ominous stairway that led to the basement of this multi-faceted building, and there in all its splendor was "The Carnegie Lyceum Theatre". . . . a little gem of a theater if you happened to be a spelunker. It seated two hundred people and also served as a workshop for those of us who were studying scenic design, directing, and other allied arts.

The first day of rehearsal we would start with a reading. Then came the days of blocking, followed by two weeks of intensive rehearsal. Finally we were sent downstairs to the Lyceum for three days of dress rehearsal, going over and over and over the play with that legendary teacher, Charles Jehlinger, who put the final touches on it. Then came the big day! The performance! And we were no longer virgins. We had appeared on Broadway! The following day, the applause still ringing in our ears, we started to learn a new play. Six months of this and somehow we took on the veneer of actors.

Although Mr. Diestal was the vice president of the school, it was really in the hands of Mr. Jehlinger. It was a partnership made in heaven . . . like the nice guy/bad guy the police use in their Mutt and Jeff syndrome. Mr. Jehlinger's tenure at the Academy must have been well over fifty years, as Edward G. Robinson, who was in the A. A. D. A. class of 1913, told me that Mr. Jehlinger was already elderly when *he* was a student. When I was there, he was a very vigorous old gentleman. Since he always simply emerged in our basement theatre, and since we never actually saw him go down or come back up, it was assumed that he did it by boat, à la the sewers of Paris.

My first encounter with the great man came when I was cast in the first play of the Senior year as a juvenile in a domestic comedy about just plain folks, aptly titled *Broken Dishes*.* The nervous cast members were sent down to the basement theatre like so many sacrificial lambs to await

---

Broken Dishes: It was in this play, starring Donald Meek, that Bette Davis made her Broadway debut—Ritz Theatre, November 1929.

his arrival. We were arranged in a semicircle on the stage, clutching our scripts in our sweaty little hands. Suddenly we were aware of the presence of a broad little man wearing huge round glasses. He was scuttling down the aisle looking like a well-dressed crab. He came to rest with his head sitting on the edge of the stage (What a temptation to go bowling!). In my two years of working under Mr. Jehlinger I never once saw him use those temporary little wooden stairs at the side of the stage. When he wanted to make a point, to get close to us—since we had no orchestra pit—he would invariably walk down front, rest his chin on the stage, cup both ears and peer up at us through his owl-like eyes. Most of the time, however, he would prowl the theatre like an alley cat, his booming, cutting, hissing voice coming at us from the damnedest places in that darkened theatre.

I had a sense of foreboding. I didn't have long to wait. Suddenly, from the back of the theatre, we heard, "Mr. Baxter, will you please make yourself ready to enter?" We waited for Baxter, whoever that might be. We'd been together for some time now and never was there a Baxter in the class. "Come, boy, the first rule of the theatre is never keep a director waiting."

Baxter? We looked around. Somehow I realized that Baxter was me! Mr. Jehlinger, like my father, was one of those people who could not remember names. Garson Kanin, who was in the class with me, became Ganson Danson, for example. Another classmate, Hume Cronyn, was Human Crone. So, trying not to be an eager beaver, I walked across the stage to the two chairs that indicated the doorway.

"Baxter!" He omitted the "Mr." when he was irked. "Where does it say for you to walk across the Bartons' living room? Why are you suddenly on the inside of the door?" He chuckled to himself and muttered almost unintelligibly, "Don't they have doors in Cleveland?" How did he know my home town?

By now he had reached the stage and was again leaning his chin on it and cupping his ears. "Go ahead, Baxter."

I realized I should have gotten to the indicated door by walking around in back of the indicated living room. I stood behind the two chairs and wiped my feet.

"Mr. Baxter, what are you doing with your feet? Some kind of war dance? . . ." There was more, but it was muttered. I couldn't understand his gibberish.

"Well, Mr. Jehlinger, rather than just stand there, I thought I'd wipe my feet in case it was raining."

"I don't see anything about rain in this scene, boy. This is not a play about a hurricane. C'mon, son, are you trying to stop the sun from shining?" The word "son" he pronounced with an "sh," as "shun." Then more chuckling and garbled words. He was more than amused at his own jokes.

"Mr. Jehlinger, I just—"

"Shun, never argue with the director. The eggs do not teach the hen." (Mild chuckle.) "Go back, boy! . . . Now, Mr. Baxter, will you please make yourself ready to enter? Come, boy, the first rule of the theatre is never keep the director waiting. . . ."

"From the last place we started from?" I asked. I was thoroughly confused.

"No," he said, in patient exasperation, "you can stand there if you want. You told the cab driver to take you to that spot only three feet from the two chairs on the stage of this theatre. But, as Mr. Johnson, you came all the way from Pittsburgh! Come now, silly Mr. Baxter from Pittsburgh who doesn't talk to doors. Which one are you?" He chuckled and waited.

What was he talking about? What did he mean? Was this the director I'd heard so much about? I tried to sort it out. "Well, sir, as Mr. Baxter, I'm me."

"I'm glad," said the great director, "because you left Mr. Johnson outside, where it isn't raining, playing a scene with his feet and making animal noises."

By now I was filled with impotent, bewildered rage. Then, suddenly, it came to me. It was his way of telling me that I had walked across the stage, which was now an indicated set of a living room, and had walked through the front door and had anticipated the rain, which was to follow in Act Three. Mr. Johnson was really me, silly amateur Mr. Baxter, out of one Jim Backus. Sounds complicated, but not if done right. It's as simple as driving the *Twentieth Century Limited* on a teaspoonful of coal. . . . Oh, my God, he had *me* doing it! I made that entrance twenty-seven times. That's the way it went. Once on *Hurry Sundown*, on location in Louisiana, in an ancient courthouse on a day when it was 106 degrees outside and who knows what the temperature was inside that musty building with all those hot "brute" lights shining on me, the director, Otto Preminger, had me do an involved courtroom scene, in which I played a lawyer, twenty-eight times!

Both Jehlinger and Preminger operated like the Marines, where the training is so tough it's a relief to go into battle! But it worked! They got results. I realize now that Mr. Jehlinger somehow made it happen. He took that class of twenty bright-eyed, dewy-faced boys and girls who had trembled their way down into that basement theater and molded them into actors who, in three days' time, were able to perform before a tough, show-wise Broadway audience.

This Is Henny . . .

The Rosetta stone should live so long! Move over, Tut-ankhamen, you've got a roommate! Happy boys are winning ponies! And now, for the two-million-dollar trivia question on "Who dat who say 'Who dat' when I say, 'Who dat?!' " Where did Jim Backus get the voice of *Mr. Magoo*? Don't be an idiot, shun. The egg doesn't tell the hen!

Nothing Today

Here I was, all alone now . . . me! Jim Backus of Cleveland, now Manhattan, graduate of the best drama school in the country. Kate was gone, back to Cleveland to marry for the second time, the groom-to-be Joseph W. Spencer, engineer, and my father's young partner. So here I was, in my three-dollar-a-week room in a fleabag in Greenwich Village. I lay back on my bed and stretched. At that moment Katie's old whistling teakettle did its number. My room was so small I could reach out and get a cup, throw in a tea bag, pour in the boiling water—all without leaving my humble cot. My room was so small the mice were all hunchbacked. But it was air-conditioned. The manager blew in the key-hole. . . . But it was so small, you had to go out in the hall to change your mind.*

Hold it! That was all right for the Madison Club on a Saturday night. But, coming from a graduate of the American Academy of Dramatic Arts! I looked up the window. Yes, that's right, up the window. My room was in an air shaft and got about fifteen minutes of light a day. My room was all right if you happened to be a mole! I waited for a

*Thank you, Henny Youngman.

nonexistent laugh. Then I decided to do what every actor has to do—try to get a job. I leaped up, dressed carefully, stared at myself in the mirror, tilted my brown snap-brim hat to a more rakish angle, and exited my room.

I headed for the Penn Astor drugstore. Everyone knew about the Penn Astor. It was the rendezvous for young aspiring actors and actresses. It was on the southwest corner of the Hotel Astor and could be reached from a street entrance. They came here to find out from each other who was casting, was anyone holding auditions, and which agents were seeing people. Most of the time was spent by those kids in job hunting. They were in and out of the drugstore eight or nine times a day. The management kept hoping that someday they might take their trade elsewhere, but the embryonic Barrymores felt they were gracing this apothecary shop with their presence. Besides, it was in the middle of everything, and it had nice clean johns and eight telephone booths.

On this particular morning most of the counter space, the booths, and the telephones were occupied. Some of these young would-be actors were nursing a nickel cup of coffee or a Coke or eating a communal muffin. They all knew each other and there was a great sense of sharing.

I sat down and ordered a Coke and started to read my *Actors' Cues*, which told who was casting and where. The kids in the drugstore were reading or sharing the same paper. The fact that it was mostly inaccurate had never hurt its sales, for actors live on hope, and who cares if most of the tips were false. I looked around the noisy room. The kids were rushing in and out of the two large doors, shouting to the room at large, "Don't go over to the National! It's strictly a cattle call!" Another one complained to the room, "You know what's lousy? You can't get a job unless you belong to Equity, and you can't belong to Equity until you have a job!"

Then a hysterical young man came storming in. "Listen! Everybody!" We listened. "They're casting a road company

at the Booth! For a juvenile!" All the boys started to dash
out. "Wait a minute! You have to go through an agent!"

The boys started for the phone booths—not me, though.
I didn't have an agent. Anyway, all I need is my diploma,
I thought. Wait till they see that! Who needs a road com-
pany anyway? I decided instead to go and see some agents
I had heard about.

I crossed Forty-fourth Street at the Booth Theatre, where
that musical smash *Everybody's Welcome!* was still playing, to 234 West Forty-fourth Street, the Sardi building,
which was directly across the street. I opened the door
and trod along its badly lit, linoleum-floored hall, on each
side of which were office doors with frosted glass windows
that looked as if they belonged in a private-eye movie.
Although it wasn't the most elegant building, I knew from
the underground that it housed some pretty big agents plus
a few producers, notably those partners John Houseman
and Orson Welles. Who cares what the building is like, I
thought, as long as they get you a job. I had been warned
that Sara Ensign couldn't get anybody a job. They said she
hadn't booked anything since the Last Supper, with the
original cast. Still, it wouldn't hurt to try.

I walked up the stairs and stopped before Room 405. The
letters on the door proclaimed:

SARA ENSIGN   THEATRICAL AGENT   ALSO C.P.A.

I opened the door and entered her office. Once you entered
her office, you entered her office. That was it . . . no waiting
room, no reception area. Miss Ensign was seated behind a
dilapidated, simulated oak desk which took up the entire
office space, so that your fore was in the office and your
aft was in the hall. She looked up from her figuring and
shook her brassy, badly hennaed head. I looked at her hopefully. Then I took a deep breath and said, "Thought you
might know of something I'd be right for!" I stood up to
her like a real pro.

"Nothing today," she said, going back to her figuring. I

started to hand her my diploma. She just stared at me. "Kid," she said, waving me out, "that and a nickel will get you on the subway!"

I remember leaving the Sardi building and walking toward Broadway. Where next? The name of Uncle Len's friend, Leland Hayward, came to mind, but I dismissed that. It was silly to try without an introduction or a good part under my belt. That went for the other classy theatre agents, like Brisco and Goldsmith, for example. I'd heard about them and about that lady agent in the Times building, Jane Broder. She handled hot people like Jane Wyatt and Rosalind Russell, for whom she had actually gotten a movie contract no less. I wouldn't even get my foot in the door without experience. But where would I get that?

I had some hopes of getting in to see Churchill Brown. They said he'd see anybody. They also said he was great if you wanted to play stock on the moon. Still, you never could tell. I made a right on Forty-fifth Street. One-forty-five. There it was.

Churchill Brown's theatrical empire consisted of two nondescript rooms covered with vintage posters featuring his clients, most of whom had gone to the great greenroom in the sky. It was as if it were frozen in time. I took a deep breath and walked in. Everyone knew that Leslie Brown really ran his brother's business. When I walked in, Leslie was seated at his shabby desk in the anteroom, talking on the phone. He took my name and motioned me to sit on the bench on the other side of the boiling, airtight, dust-laden room, and went back to his telephone conversation. I could hear him complaining in a sibilant Southern accent, not helped by his ill-fitting dentures. As I listened, I waited for one of them to leap from his mouth. When he lisped, they clicked like a demented flamenco dancer.

The buzzer on his desk buzzed three times. Pushing his plate back in place with his tongue and, as though he were a majordomo at the court of St. James, he intoned in a voice of thunder, "Churchill will see you now!" I remember how

nervous I was as I walked in to see his brother. Who knows?
I was hopeful. Maybe he knows something.

Churchill was a corpulent, bald capon of a man. He was
dressed in a heavy white linen suit, which I understood he
wore the year round. He was covered with antique jewelry.
I had heard the unfounded rumor that he was the proud
possessor of a combination penis and vagina. But, the way
he looked, it was unlikely that he'd ever find a recipient
for either. At this moment he was sitting at his desk strok-
ing and kissing a huge white angora cat. After a pause he
lisped liquidly, without bothering to look up, "Nothing
today, son."

I held out my diploma. Churchill looked up and eyed it
as though it were a cobra. He leaped up, dropping his cat,
and danced around me on tippytoes. He circled the room,
keeping well out of the way of my diploma. The cat reacted
by doing a leap worthy of Nijinsky to the top of a filing
cabinet, hissing venomously and striking out with its little
lethal claws.

I just stood there. I must confess I was confused.

"Leslie!" screamed Churchill. "A process server!!"

Leslie came scrambling in and, before I knew what had
happened, he snookered me through the door and out into
the hall.

I consulted my copious notes. Merv Samuels' office. The
Brill building. Forty-seventh and Broadway. Mr. Samuels,
I had heard, booked anything, including conventions, fairs,
and industrials. My hopes were high.

The sign on the door read:

MERVIN SAMUELS

THEATRICAL REPRESENTATION

Myra Samuels, wife and secretary, was deep in conversation on the phone. I stood in front of her desk and
waited . . . endlessly. I remembered that the kids referred
to her as "the yenta with the electric tongue." She looked

up for a moment and said, "Sorry, kid. Nothing today," and went back to her clacking.

Just then the door opened and Mr. Samuels popped into the room. He was an energetic little man who bounced around the room as if on a spring. He exuded an air of dishonest enthusiasm. I held out my diploma and started to speak.

He took it and gave it a cursory glance. "Hoo hah!! Look, Mrs. Victrola Record," he said to his wife, who was still clacking away on the phone. "A diploma! John Barrymore should live so long!" He handed back my diploma and, as he hopped to his private office he called over his shoulder, *"Mazel tov!"*

I could think of only one more place to go, Cliff Smith's. For twenty-five cents a week you could climb the stairs to his Broadway cubbyhole and read the latest casting tips on his bulletin board and drink all the coffee you could hold.

Cliff, like most agents, was never off the phone. A very skinny man? Tall? Small? I never knew—he never left his chair. I paid my two bits, poured myself a paper cup of coffee, and hung around talking to the other out-of-work actors and hoped someone would come in who knew something.

It was a bad time of year. By April it was too late for a job playing summer stock and much too early for any local activity. The Broadway season started in the fall. All that was left was the subway circuit—Brooklyn, the Bronx, Staten Island, etc.—cheap revivals in a group of theatres that could be reached by subway. Wee and Leventhal handled those. Week after week I tried for that, and all I heard was:

"Nothing today."

It was time to face facts, take a personal inventory. I had been job-hunting every day for more than two months . . . nothing! Sure, there were a few interviews, along with other aspirants, but nothing came of it. Day after day of those torturous rounds. But was I discouraged? Hell, no! I wasn't

experienced enough for that. At that age, optimism and
energy are high, and I ran on regular, unleaded, and premium. "Who knows?" I told myself every morning. "This
might be the day."

There was no more money from Dad, who reminded
me that things on the home front weren't that hot. After
all, we were in the midst of a Depression. The week before, a Shalimar-soaked ten-dollar bill had fluttered out of
Mother's latest letter. And that was about it. I was broke,
tapped out. But so was everyone else. Dad wanted me to
come home for the summer, but somehow I couldn't bring
myself to say yes. I had to keep trying.

I thumbed through my dog-eared notebook, which contained the list of producers and agents. Alongside their
names were notes. "Nothing today" . . . "Come back in
the fall" . . . "Leave photos". . . . And, believe it or not, that
old saw, "Don't call us, we'll call you." I noticed at the
bottom of the last page a listing for "The Gray Stevens
Agency." Where the hell did that come from? Then I remembered, of course! That kid in the Katharine Cornell
Company, Tyrone Power. He tipped me off. Come to think
of it, the handsome son of a bitch owes me ninety cents
from that dinner last night at Ralph's. I'd better get it back
or there'll be no dinner tonight!

Gray Stevens, yes! I recalled it was a modeling agency.
No, not what you're thinking. Not a place where those
leggy broads, who carried their gear in hatboxes, lolled
between assignments of posing for *Vogue* and *Harper's
Bazaar*. Gray Stevens, as Ty had pointed out, cast people
for magazines like *True Story*, *True Confessions*, *True
Detective*, to pose for stills to illustrate the stories. There
was, he told me, plenty of work in those tacky pulp magazines that were owned mostly by one Bernarr Macfadden.
Mr. Macfadden was an ancient elf who called attention to
himself and his magazines by doing wild publicity stunts
like parachute jumping out of an airplane wearing only a

diaper (he and Gandhi had the same tailor). Best of all, they paid well, sometimes as much as ten dollars a shot! I took off!

The Gray Stevens hiring hall was an enormous room completely devoid of furniture—a device to discourage loitering. On the far side of the room, underneath a huge picture of F. D. R. superimposed on an American flag, were three frosted windows side by side. They would open from time to time and a man would stick his head out and bellow something. The room was packed to capacity with every type, size, and hue of the human race. There were whites, blacks, and Orientals; midgets, giants, and dwarfs. The entire scene was reminiscent of Ellis Island at the turn of the century with its huddled masses. I recognized some of the faces from the Penn Astor drugstore.

Suddenly one of the windows opened and a head popped out. Then its voice barked, "One Filipino houseboy!"

Five little men pushed their way through and stepped forward.

"You," yelled the head as its arm appeared and pointed, "go get your voucher!" Then the voice continued, "One English major!"

Two British types fought their way forward and one was chosen.

"And one blond, fat-assed whore!"

I watched as a fat, dark-haired lady pulled a blond wig from her carryall. She slapped it on her head and elbowed her way forward.

"Okay! Window two and get your voucher."

He pointed. "You, Jerry Hausner, come in here a minute!"

It was the boy next to me. He started to push his way out.

The head withdrew and the window was slammed shut.

"Who was that?" I asked Jerry, whom I knew from the Penn Astor drugstore.

"No big deal," he told me. "He's my uncle. Probably

wants me to run an errand or something. Want to meet him?"

"Wow!"

I followed Jerry to a back door. This was too easy. There had to be a catch someplace.

By now we had reached a door that led to the inner sanctum. Jerry quickly slipped in, beckoning me to follow. We entered a tiny, airless office. It contained only a chair and a desk, which was completely covered with a snow of notes, all sorts of photographs, and a telephone. Behind the desk sat Jerry's Uncle Al, a fat, red-faced, very harassed casting man. The phone was ringing. The phone was *always* ringing. Al picked it up.

"Yeah," he barked. "Who? Gerald Ford?* Gerry? Listen, they need a World War doughboy over at Van Dams. Get over there on the double!" He hung up, pointed at Jerry, and said, "You saved me a phone call. I need you to run over to—"

Jerry interrupted him. "Listen, Uncle Al, first I want you to meet my pal Jim Backus."

The casting man, out of habit, looked me up and down.

He turned to pick up his insistently ringing phone, listened for a moment, said, "Hold it!" and put it down on its side.

"Where were we? Oh, yes." He stopped and stared at me again. "Got any pictures?"

"Oh, yes," I replied eagerly, "brand-new portraits, back at the hotel."

"Not heads!" Al yelled impatiently. "Beefcake! Nudes! Nothing on but maybe a jock strap."

I threw Jerry an accusing look as Al continued nonstop.

"There's an African shot coming up," he mumbled to himself. Then he brightened. "You know something? You're pretty tall. Right! Dark eyes, a wig, some Egyptian number-

---

*Gerald Ford: When he was a young man in the 1930s, he was a commercial model. . . . Incidentally, he later became President.

eight makeup, a bone in your nose, and you'll make one hell of a Watusi!''

For a frightening split second I saw my father reading a magazine and coming across a picture of the fruit of his loins—for whom he had gotten an expensive education— posing as a cannibal.

It was time to go home.

The Homecoming

Talk about coming home on your shield! Here I was, clumping along on the Pennsylvania Turnpike at two A.M. on a beautiful June night. . . . Three-hundred-seventy-five miles . . . point of no return . . . e.t.a. seven A.M., Cleveland bus terminal.

I was occupying the only seat left on this aluminum behemoth. When I boarded, there were two seats: one on the aisle, Greyhound's finest, and across, toward the rear, the dreaded seat over the wheel—anathema to any experienced bus traveler. As I was just about to put my derrière down on the aisle seat, I noticed standing alongside of me, and just about to do the same, a very distinguished-looking elderly black gentleman. Every eye was on us. The entire passenger list was staring me down as if to say, "How dare a snot-nosed kid like you take that seat and force that distinguished-looking black gentleman to have to sit over the wheel!"

I mimed a "Sorry" worthy of Stan Laurel and wrapped myself around the auxiliary tire. The man in front turned around and gave me a "Thank you from all of us" moue. Still perplexed, I asked him who the distinguished-looking old black gentleman was. He shot me an Oliver Hardy patient look. "That's Alan Clay Hoskins' father!"

I nodded, "But of course!" and settled back on my tire just in time to get a fusillade of gravel as the driver swerved off the road. Once again I prodded the self-appointed cruise director and asked, "Excuse me, but who is Alan Clay Hoskins?"

The man did a Macready* and then really let it out. "Alan Clay Hoskins is really Farina!† And that's Farina's father!" he said proudly. "This bus gets *all* the celebrities!"

I muttered a very contrite "Oh." I was about to tell him that I, too, was in show business and flash my diploma, when the bus driver turned off all but the emergency "good night" lights, which seemed to say, "All right, you two necking in the back, get on with it. You've only got twenty miles till fruit inspection."

I settled back as best I could and closed my eyes. The *rat-a-tat-tat* of the boulders beating a tattoo on my rear had a somewhat distorted, lulling effect. I was asleep, yet I was somehow aware of where I was. What a difference, I thought, between traveling with Uncle Len on the *Twentieth Century* with that snow-white napery and the Haig and Haig pinch, and this broken-down bus with Old Drum blend in a paper bag that a couple of passengers near me were slugging.

I guess I must have fallen asleep. I was awakened by soft moaning behind me. Thank God the couple in the rear had made it. When they finally simmered down, I once again drifted into a hazy sleep. Again I was awakened by soft little moans. That couple in the rear was well into twozies. I mentally congratulated them and slept the rest of the way.

*Macready: The great nineteenth-century English actor famous for his meaningful pauses.

†Farina: The adorable little black boy in the original Hal Roach *Our Gang* comedies.

Cleveland! Home! What a surprise! As I disembarked, there was Katie—my tall, elegant, darling sister—waiting in the station to greet me. I figured she was there to protect her ten-dollar investment that got me home. She must have needed every cent for her trousseau, as Dear Old Dad wasn't about to spring for a second one. It was nice of Kate to meet me, as it was an hour's ride in a private car from the downtown bus station to Bratenahl. If she hadn't, it would have meant another bus ride.

They pushed their way through the front door in their eagerness to greet me, Wa Wa, Mother, Dad, and his new dog, an overweight cocker spaniel named Duchess. They were very happy to see me. It was good to be home.

It was a fine summer. I saw some friends, played some golf, and studied some plays. It was a good thing that I was back home as, in the midst of all the summer festivities, my appendix ruptured!

Several years back, when I was seventeen, during the Easter vacation from University School, I somehow became a part of the distinguished Robert McLaughlin stock company as an extra in a play called *White Cargo*. All I had to do was to get into a full black makeup and a loincloth and run across the stage brandishing a whip and muttering gibberish, which was supposed to be some African language or other. Hardly *Hamlet*! They gave me a nail in the basement to use as a dressing room, and it was there that I "received" after my performance, greeting my awed friends and serving after-theatre libations out of paper Lily cups behind the furnace.

The McLaughlin company was going full blast that summer when, hoping that he'd remember me, I decided to call Mr. McLaughlin and ask for an interview. It was almost too easy. He saw me, I read for him, and I got the part—a bit in *Peppermint Heart*, understudy to the juvenile, and assistant stage manager—twenty-five dollars a week!! I was ecstatic! I could pay my debt to Katie and start saving for my return to Broadway. There was no way Dad could help me. The Depression had gotten to him, too.

The third day of rehearsal, through no fault of my own, I was late. As I dashed toward the stage door, I was met by an irate stage manager, who followed me in, shouting, "Where the hell have you been? We skipped your scene and went right into the third act! Everyone is fit to be tied, and Mr. McLaughlin is not too pleased, either!"

"Gee, I couldn't help it." And it was true. "My alarm never went off."

"Mr. M. wants to see you, Backus!" He pointed to the lobby stairs. "Up in his office! And right away."

Oh, my God! I thought. He's going to fire me! In my terror I spun around rapidly and almost knocked down Miss Cahill, our character actress. I apologized and steadied her. She smiled flirtatiously up at me. I started my death march down the little stage stairs, rushed through the aisle into the lobby and up the stairs to the door marked "Office," and knocked. "Come in!" he bellowed.

Mr. McLaughlin was an austere man with fierce hawk-like features and eyes that could pierce an armored truck. He spoke with authority, and every sentence was a pronouncement. He wore a full stage makeup, had a dazzling set of false choppers, and a scalp doily that defied description. He didn't get dressed in the morning . . . he got assembled. There were rumors that there was a Mrs. McLaughlin, but if there was, he must have kept her under house arrest, locked up in the jelly closet.

I entered. The office was a clutter of props, posters, and furniture from past productions. It made David Belasco's office seem monastic. I approached his huge junk-covered desk, which reposed on a platform, and waited.

"Come here, son." He waved me toward him. I came as close as possible.

"Yes, sir!" I said, standing stiffly at attention in front of his desk.

"Would you do anything to make this play a success?"

"Oh, yes, sir!" I said eagerly.

"All right," said Mr. McLaughlin. "You know Miss Cahill, who plays the mother-in-law?"

"Yes, sir," I said. "She's a fine actress, sir."

"Yes," said my producer. "She's a great actress. But she's also a very nervous lady, and there's only one way to simmer her down. So, Backus, before the opening night, just slip up to her room at the inn and give her a little old mercy hump. It won't hurt you, and it'll do her a lot of good."

I froze. I was unable to speak. Without another look at me, he went back to his work. I stood there for a moment and finally managed to get to the door and out.

I can't do that, I thought. That's awful! How could I? No way would I . . . and God was on my side. I didn't have to, because the very next night my appendix burst!

It really wasn't funny. Fortunately, my sister Katie and my brother-in-law-to-be, Jock, came to fetch me after rehearsal. They found me on the dressing room floor unconscious. A burst appendix even now is a very serious business, on top of which I got pneumonia. I was in that hospital forever. What a great hospital! Believe it or not, they ran it for the patient! My last week in the hospital was a ball. The nurses made my room a hangout, a sanctuary where they could sneak a cigarette or a shot of illicit gin before a date or, better yet, a place where they could bitch about their patients.

And so I was brought home by Katie to recuperate. Mother and Dad had long since taken off for the Gaspé Peninsula. My beautiful mother, whom I adored, had a difficult time resisting a trip, a party, a shopping spree, or a drink, and all she had to do was give my father a bourbon and one of her smiles and he'd follow her anywhere. But that was all right. I'd do fine. I was okay, really I was. I was used to being in that house with Katie and Wa Wa and Olive.

Actually, I was happy Mother and Pop were able to get away.

The bursting of my appendix also meant the bursting of my burgeoning career. As soon as they got back from their trip, Pop called a high-level meeting in the sunroom. As usual, he presided from our ancient ornate wicker chaise longue which we called "King Tut's tomb." He and Mother looked absolutely smashing—tan, healthy, fresh from the Gaelic charm of the Gaspé Peninsula. It was good to have them back. Pop called the meeting into session and explained that what was to be discussed could be resolved by a show of hands. Olive, as usual, gave Wa Wa her raise-of-the-hand proxy and retired to the kitchen to abstain with a few strategic shots of gin.

Back in his chambers, Pop was winding up his summation. ". . . and so it all boils down to this. The family exchequer is now down to the danger point and, until we weather this economic storm—which that man in the White House assures us will be soon—I think we'll have to reef our sails and stay to leeward. Which means, Jim, there is no appropriation from the family till for you to return to New York. Has anybody got any suggestions?"

Wa Wa looked up from her lethal Old-fashioned and took the floor. "I don't see why Jimmy can't get a job right here in Cleveland. I vote that he stay right here at home."

Mr. Chin snarled a second. Kate nodded her assent, and then she and Pop went into a caucus. We could hear Pop saying, "Listen, Kate, some of your former in-laws might help us out by getting Jim a job to tide him over."

Kate snapped her fingers. "I know just the right one. I'll call him tomorrow and have lunch with him. I'm talking about Carl Hanna. I wonder what's coming into the Hanna Theatre. . . ."

Pop nodded. "Fine!" he said. "And I'll have a meeting with John Royal. He's head of that new company, RCA.

They own radio stations all over hell's half acre. I did him a favor when he managed the Palace Theatre," Pop said, as he winked a loaded wink. "Jim"—he turned to me— "how would you like to be a radio announcer?"

I beamed.

To make it official, Pop addressed the assembled. "May I have a show of hands? . . . All in favor? . . . Thank you. The motion is carried."

The Announcer

Being a radio announcer in 1936 (I preferred to be known as a "communicator") wasn't all that bad. Besides, I liked to think of it as a pit stop in what I was sure was going to be a long and varied career. Movie stardom and the theatre were merely being put on the back burner and, after all, being an announcer was still show business.

As with everything else, you had to know the angles. The second week I was on staff at WTAM, the NBC outlet for Cleveland, I heard that there were to be auditions for a spokesman for "Stars Over the Great Lakes," a big network show, and since it was sponsored by Standard Oil of Ohio, they were doing it right. Each of us was to be taken up at night, separately, in the Goodyear blimp and told to describe the 1936 Cleveland Exposition below. Knowing full well what it would look like from the air, I wrote it all out in advance and memorized it. It contained such flowery phrases as, "From ten thousand feet the lights look like so many jewels in the diadem of freedom" and "The Cuyahoga River is cascading eagerly into the welcoming bosom of Lake Erie." (Twenty-five years later this river was so polluted it distinguished itself by catching fire.) Anyway, I got the job and was off and running.

Being a radio announcer at that time was indeed a glamorous, prestigious profession. The pay, considering the fact that we were in the maw of a Depression, wasn't too bad, and I had no real expenses, since I was living at home.

WTAM Cleveland was a powerful 50,000-watt station and was one of six "O and O" stations. "O and O" meant that it was owned and operated by NBC. NBC operated in a paramilitary manner with overtones of the British Foreign Office, and we were the cadets. Our role models were such hallowed names as Milton J. Cross, Alois Havrilla, and André Baruch—these were giants who walked the earth—not to mention Del Sharbutt, Harry Von Zell, and of course the most thunderous of them all, Westbrook Van Voorhis, the mere mention of whose name stayed eagles in their flight. His voice could shatter a shaving mug at twenty paces—"Today, as it must to all men, death came to . . ." When Van Voorhis said good-bye to you, it meant that you *were* somebody—but good-bye already! I can still see those fan pictures that I sent away for of these cupped-ear greats. Each one held the script in his left hand and with his right he cupped his ear so he could hear and revel in the mellifluousness of his voice. Much later I learned that listening to your own voice was a no-no at any good acting school.

There were eight on the announcers staff, and I was the only unmarried one. I was the only announcer there without a wife who wanted him home nights and away from the temptations found in the nightclubs from which we did our remotes. So I got my share of remotes, to say nothing of girls. A "remote" is any broadcast originating outside the studio: a speech from an auditorium, a sporting event, and of course, the dance band remotes originating from such fleshpots as "The Vogue Room from high atop the Hollenden Hotel," "The 4300 Club from high atop 4300," "The Lotus Gardens from high atop Playhouse Square in downtown Cleveland," and let's not forget "The Patent Leather Club from high atop glamorous Carnegie Avenue—on Used Car Row!" We also had two more dance band remotes at noon, yes, noon! "From the exotic Golden Pheasant it's Isham Jones and his Orchestra. And now, stepping mikeside is perky Peggy Haley to ask the musical question, 'Who?'" And "From the Beach Room of the Wade Park Manor it's the music of Austin Wiley. And now, tripping mikeside is Sally Summers to ask the musical question, 'Why Do I Love You?'" Notice the "high atop" billing is gone. It was used only late at night. The noon remotes were more practical and down-to-earth for the ladies who lunched together and danced with each other.

When I was a child, all announcers wore tuxedos while on duty. I remember as a lad of fourteen my embarrassment when my mother came upon me in the bathroom and surprised me as I stood in front of the mirror in my father's tuxedo with both ears cupped intoning, "The March of Time!"

The reign of the announcer as *numero uno* was fairly short-lived. The advent of the comedians who reigned supreme demanded announcers who were more informal and relaxed. They utilized them as their straight men, much as Johnny Carson does with Ed McMahon. At that time it was Jimmy Wallington for Eddie Cantor, Don Wilson for Jack Benny, Harry Von Zell for Fred Allen and later for Burns and Allen. Von Zell was one of the few who bridged the gap from radio to television.

I came into broadcasting when the tuxedo was no longer *de rigueur*. However, the uniform of the day was a banker's stripe or a charcoal-gray three-piece suit with a conservative shirt and tie. We were told when we were hired that we were to be more of a friend, more of a counselor than an elocutionist. After all, we had a real studio audience.

We had a lounge where we kept a change of clothes and where the ticker tapes were, over which clicked the news, weather, hog and grain prices (very important, as Ohio was and still is an agrarian state), plus the latest in sports and entertainment. There was a cubbyhole for each announcer containing his schedule and copy. The lounge reminded me of the faculty room for dons I had often seen in English movies. Oh, how I envied an old timer (all of twenty-seven) who did the six o'clock news. At five-fifty he would rush in, rip off the tape sputtering out of the top of the ticker, grab a handful of that, plus some wheat and grain averages, plus the weather (this, too, was very important to the farmer) and, clutching these, he would spill out fifteen minutes of the complete goings-on. It seems strange today, with newscasters getting a million dollars a year and fancy-talking weather forecasters not too far behind, that we used to fight *not* to do the weather, even though it paid an extra five bucks.

At about this time, the ebullient disc jockey was invented. Now *he* had a foot in the door! We legitimate announcers had nothing but scorn and contempt for those loud, brassy, conniving charlatans, those jocks who were coming up fast on the inside. All of the owned and operated stations, most of the affiliated stations, and the super independents banned those players of Victrola records. So the disc jockey had to take his shoddy wares elsewhere, which gave birth to the "mom and pop" stations. These feisty little underground stations operated without the sanction of Uncle Sam and subsisted on payola. I remember as late as 1973 I was plugging an album I'd made and was to be interviewed on an underground station in Chicago. I was met by the program manager, a shifty-looking character who drove me by a devious route so that I would never be able to find the place again. The radio station itself was a seedy hotel suite. The actual broadcasting equipment—turntables, etc.—was in the bathroom. And where did I sit? Of course!

Radio, and for that matter television, has always had payola, or should we say "the barter system"? I forget what my actual take-home pay was, but it was the perks, the goodies, I was interested in. For example, the station would book in a horrible hillbilly act. (No one ever dreamed then

Jimmy at ten months—"in my first convertible."

Caught in the act!

Richard Burton and I cementing public relations on the set of *Ice Palace*.

Back row: (left to right) Walter Pratt, Hunter Van Sicklin, Gorman Dawes, Pearus Hasse, Corning Chisholm, Charles Tomkins. Middle row: Minnie Tomkins, Janet Mass, Edith Sheridan, Ruby Hawkins, Helen Johnson, Virginia Wick, Elissa Strong, Peggy Baker. Front: Me and Sidney Morton competing in the mumbly peg invitational!

Somewhere along the way I lost it.

"The Old Vic." Napoleon said "In every soldier's knapsack is a field marshal's baton." Inside mine, was my lunch.

Jim and the late great Jimmy Demaret making a golf movie at MGM.

"Bombshell"—Mother, Kate, me, and the terrible tempered Mr. Chin.

Ed Wynn's seventieth birthday. Rear: (left to right) Jack Palance, Red Skelton, unknown, unknown, me, Keenan Wynn. Front: Paul Stewart, Jose Ferrer, Rosemary Clooney, director Ralph Nelson, Henny, unknown, Mrs. Sharlee Wynn, and Mrs. Edna Skelton.

Henny's Bette and the real Bette Davis in *The Star*.

Garbo by Henny the sculptress.

Henny the model!

Henny the actress!

"What's so funny about Cleveland?"

Jim as Hubert Updyke III on
The Alan Young Radio Show
later to become Thurston
Howell III on *Gilligan's Island*.

A scene from the Twentieth Century-Fox production *Father Was a Fullback*.

The Iron Man starring Jeff Chandler, on the far left; Joyce Holden; Rock Hudson in his second picture; Evelyn Keyes (Scarlett O'Hara's younger sister).

Jim and Jimmy Dean kidding around between set-ups while filming *Rebel Without a Cause*.

Kirk Douglas (Goodwin) and Jim (Gooch) in *Top Secret Affair*, a Warner Brothers production.

Joan Davis and I in a delicate moment on *I Married Joan*.

". . . You walked through his horse!" Cast photo of *Our Town* including: Back row extreme left: John Beal. Second from right: producer Martha Scott (who played "Emily" in original cast). Front row second from left: Mildred Natwick. Then, fourth from left: Henry Fonda, me, John Randolph, and Irene Tedrow.

Our first date . . . and it's been
Hearts and Flowers all the way!

Pop and Daisy vacationing—1953.

Jim and Leslie Caron in her first movie *The Man with a Cloak*.

"My advice is: pay the two dollars!"

Susan St. James, Henny, and me on location in Italy at the colosseum making *Magic Carpet* (tune in any time after 3:00 A.M. . . !)

Buddy Hackett, Jim, and Mickey Rooney in *Mad, Mad, Mad, Mad World*—"Oooh that tastes good!"

On the *Merv Griffin Show*: (left to right) Eddie Albert, Jim, Dave Garroway, director John Rich, and Merv. Jim is telling the Feen-a-Mint joke.

Mike Douglas and Jim on Mike's show telling the Feen-a-Mint joke to the hard of hearing.

On *PM East*—July 1962. Left to right: songwriter Sammy Cahn, writer-director Abe Burroughs, unknown, Mike Wallace, unknown, Henny, and me.

Jim and musical director Walter Scharff doing the songs for *Magoo's Christmas Carol.*

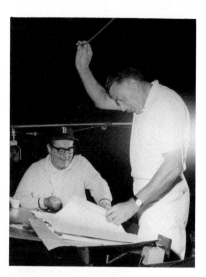

We even play department stores!

John Chancellor, Henny, and me on location with *The Today Show.*

Vegas—inside the gorilla suit is
another gorilla.

"But, I will say this about Vegas . . ."

Las Vegas revisited!

Debarking the Super-Chief—no planes for her. Henny's the only girl to ever have her picture on the cover of the *Railroad Guide*.

I wanted to buy the *Queen Elizabeth* for Henny, but the Cunard people wouldn't break up a set! Note Henny's lucky carpetbag!

that hillbilly music would someday sweep the world as Country Western.) I announced a show called "Chief Red Bird and His Tribe." The "Chief" made a deal with the station. He would do an hour show every week—without pay; no wampum was to exchange hands. In exchange, he would have the right to sell whatever elixir/nerve tonic/hair straightener he was pushing that year. I, on the other hand, would do the introducing and whatever commercials he had scrounged up, and, in exchange, I was permitted to make my own pitch: I would cheerfully send my personally autographed photo in exchange for a self-addressed envelope and twenty-five cents.

During my year at WTAM, a new vogue in broadcasting appeared. It was called *vox pop*, Latin for "voice of the people." It wasn't long before the station had assigned me, with a roving microphone in hand, to interview people on the street. So every day at five P.M. I would station myself in front of the terminal tower, the City Hall, the auditorium, or wherever, chatting with the people as they passed by. We brought up the issues of the day, and then each would be asked the "stumper," usually a riddle or a trick question, the winner to receive a case of P. O. C. Beer (Pride of Cleveland). P. O. C. Beer was our sponsor. We were going along just fine when I suddenly had a brainstorm. Why do the show in front of the terminal tower, or City Hall or the public square? What could they do for me?

I was beginning to connive, so I started doing shows in front of various restaurants and cocktail bars in exchange for their products—free wining and dining. If I happened to need a pair of shoes, I'd do it in front of a shoe store.

Finally I decided to go for the big one. At that time there was a tremendous theatre that had been converted into a nightclub to end all nightclubs. I did some real conniving and got a deal to do my P. O. C. Beer show right from their stage. First I interviewed the star, then several of the showgirls, in what I hoped would be an exchange of *their* products. Then, to give the show an international flavor, I decided to interview the wine steward.

The wine steward was very impressive. There weren't many of them around Cleveland in those days. He was wearing his very grand uniform-of-office, with the symbolic golden chain bearing the giant key to the wine cellar. Now, may I say a wine steward to advise the local gentry of their choice of wines with dinner was a man to be reckoned with—and I had him on *my* program! Edward R. Murrow should live so long!

The interview was going along beautifully. It was beyond my fondest expectations, as he had an imperious manner and spoke in a delightful Viennese dialect. At the start of the interview, I asked him where he had worked in the past. To my delight, he said that he had been in the households of several grand dukes and had worked in such places as the Raffles Hotel in Shanghai, Maxim's in Paris, and the Adlon Hotel in Berlin. (What he was doing in Cleveland, he never explained.) I was in seventh heaven when he added that he had served such people as Kaiser Wilhelm, Emperor Franz Josef, Bernard Baruch, and the Grand Khedive of Egypt. I had visions of my ratings soaring, my sponsor giving me a substantial bonus and putting my show on a national hookup!

I then asked him exactly what were his duties, and he pompously explained, "I am here to advise people on the correct wines to go weeth each course. Amereecans can be so—how you say?—stupeed. They, for example, want to order a claret to go weeth their sole, when I will allow them only to have a fine Chablis, wheech I personally decant. Then, for a festive occasion, I may inseest that they have weeth their glacé a beautiful champagne weeth laughter een its bouquet . . . perhaps a Lançon '28."

Suddenly it hit me! Here I was, sponsored by the P. O. C. Beer Company, and this man was talking only about wines! But, secure in the knowledge that I was master of the sit-

uation, I said, "And I'll bet to a lot of diners you recommend
that they drink P. O. C. Beer with their meal!"

There was a long pause while he glared at me and, giving
me the full Teutonic treatment, scathingly spat, "Beer ees
for peegs!"

Needless to say, I was stunned. But, recovering quickly,
I said, "Well, ha, ha, ha . . . some pigs get the best. But, sir,
you've got to admit that on a hot day with a hot dog there's
nothing better than a cold glass of beer!"

He delivered another scorcher when he said, "Beer, under
my conditions, ees slop. Eet causes gas! Dulls the taste
buds! Maybe eef you are outdoors, perhaps on a reever bank,
a seep of Heineken or a swallow of Muenchner ees per-
meesable, but that garbage P. O. C.? Never! Phooey!"

He strode away as I weakly said, "We now return you
to the station for an interlude of organ music."

And, may I tell you, your on-the-spot reporter was on-
the-spot canceled.

Surrogate Father

"Back in New York . . ."—a phrase often used by down-hearted, depressed actors.

"Back in New York!"—it could be a cry of anticipation, one of jubilation.

I was somewhere in between. It was 1938. I was back in New York, all right, after my debacle in Cleveland, but still beating the bushes of my ambiguous career. "Nothing today!" "Leave pictures." "Don't call us, we'll call you." It was almost two years later, but nothing had changed.

I found out the hard way that whatever you did outside of New York didn't mean a damn. But now I had a few bucks in my kick,* a snazzy wardrobe, and, of course, my "pocket full of dreams."

So I checked into the St. Regis, one of the most expensive hostelries in town. I'll put on a front! Beat 'em at their own game! I thought. What the hell, I'd been a success—I was a hit in "Stars Over the Great Lakes," and I had the notices to prove it. Not to mention my own radio

---

*Kick: See "grouchbag."
 Grouchbag: See "wallet."
 Wallet: See "kick."

program, *Moonlight Memories*, starring yours truly, with background music by Betty Lou Taylor and her Mighty Organ. I showed my notices to the assistant manager, who raised his smartly plucked eyebrows and said, "How nice for you." The bartender in the King Cole Room was not exactly overwhelmed, either. I showed him the picture of me, my ear cupped just like André Baruch, with Mary Lou Taylor and her Mighty Wurlitzer. All he said was, "Nice tits on the lady playing the organ," and moved the peanuts to the other end of the bar. Smart ass, I thought. Little did he know that I was going to do him some good—use his bar as my official office, just as Walter Winchell does at the Stork Club.

I showed the picture to Mervin Samuels and his wife Myra, who was still on the phone. "Look! Look, Myra, look who's back! The uptown Yankee Doodle boy with new pictures! Look, Mrs. Victrola Record!" Then to me, "Very nice. Very nice." He was more impressed than he let on. Myra put her hand over the mouthpiece and took a peek at it. "About the tuckus on the broad playing the calliope!" was all she said.

Every day I went hopefully on my rounds—more of same—and every evening I had guests at the King Cole Bar (this was the way it was done, I figured!) until that day when I was forced to leave and find digs elsewhere.

I checked out. I knew it would be close, but not that close. After paying the bill, I got two fives, a one, and some change back. That was it. Back to the Village. But first I decided to make a last grand gesture. I strode into the King Cole Bar, plunked down a five, and intoned in my best Milton J. Cross delivery to the white-coated bartender who had his back to me, "Pinch Bottle and soda, and you have one on me!" He turned around, and it was another bartender, and there still weren't any peanuts!

Miracle of miracles, I got a job the very next day! I won an audition and got a part, thanks to my ex-classmate, Garson Kanin, the play's director. I got a part! A small part, but a part! In a spring 1938 production for Broadway. Broadway! Imagine that! It was in a little play called *Hitch Your Wagon* that got mediocre notices but was sturdy enough to somehow survive until summer. Then it folded. July was a hopeless month for actors, too late for summer stock and too early for any fall season casting.

I was awakened early one morning in my five-dollar-a-week fleabag (a step up from my old three-dollar-a-week fleabag), which overlooked an air shaft which overlooked another air shaft. My bed in this furnished pilch had been nicknamed "the iron maiden" by an amorous playmate because of an iron rod that had something to do with converting this rack into a sofa that was even more uncomfortable, due to a row of huge simulated leather buttons. Sex was impossible, as the pain far outweighed the pleasure.

The knock became more insistent.

"Who's there?"

"It's me! Keenan Wynn!"

I let him in. We had just finished sharing a dressing room in the ill-fated *Hitch Your Wagon*. He looked around my humble digs. Then he opened a closet, pulled out a few shirts and some trousers, and threw them into a suitcase.

"What the hell are you doing?"

"We're going for a ride on Pop's boat."

Pop's boat turned out to be the *Sea Wynn*, a ninety-foot seagoing yacht. It carried a skipper, a steward, and a crew of three. Keenan and I were to share a stateroom, a far cry from the iron maiden.

Greeting us on the gangplank was Ed Wynn, resplendent in a captain's hat, white flannel trousers, and a blue blazer with its accompanying brass buttons.

Ed was one of the most popular stars in the country. He had starred in countless shows on Broadway, *The Perfect Fool*, *Manhattan Mary*, and *The Laugh Parade*, among them. He was just as well-known in the hinterlands, too, as he personally took the show on the road after playing New

York for a season. By the time I met Keenan, all that was pretty much behind his dad, as were the movies he had made. He was now best-known from radio. He was such a giant star that at one time he actually owned his own network.

When Ed first went on radio, he did the show from a reconstructed theatre. Ed, the band, the announcer Graham McNamee, his cast, and guest stars were all on the stage, but like all the other shows in early radio, they were separated from the audience by a huge glass curtain. The purpose of the glass curtain was to completely soundproof the working area. A sound leak from the audience would have been considered disaster. Ed couldn't tell those ridiculous jokes of his with no audience reaction, so he had the glass curtain removed. All the other comedy shows then followed suit, and that was the end of glass curtains.

Ed was sponsored by Texaco, whose "Fire Chief" gasoline sported a fire chief's hat as its logo, and Ed became known throughout the United States as "Ed Wynn, the Fire Chief" or later simply as "the Fire Chief." He was such a smash hit and his radio show was so popular that when he was on the air the nation came to a halt. The movie theatres, for example, would wheel a radio speaker out onto the stage and delay their picture till the program was over.

Ed was the last of the actor-managers, which means that he was the star, the director, the producer, the writer, the composer, and the lyricist. He had help, of course, but it was a one-man show, with Ed calling the shots.

I had met Ed just once before through Keenan, but I really got to know him during our weekend cruise. The transition from a five-dollar-a-week room to a stateroom on a ninety-foot yacht was pretty heady stuff—enough to give anyone the emotional bends. There were three other guests aboard—Ralph, a big industrialist from Muncie; a papal knight named John; and Earl Benham, Ed's tailor, a well-known figure on Broadway. With Keenan and me aboard, if nothing else, the passenger list was diversified.

There was an air of formality on the cruise as there was
with anything that involved Ed. Each evening we had a
short formal cocktail hour, then a delightful candlelight
dinner for which each of the gentlemen dressed. Actually,
Ed changed from one fascinating outfit to another as often
as one did on the S.S. *Normandie.* On the first day he made
a "welcome aboard" speech and introduced the skipper,
who assured us we were in for some good weather and fine
fishing. He added that we would be under way at dawn and
should reach the fishing grounds at noon. The skipper, we
later found out, had tried repeatedly to convince Ed to go
out where the big ones play—the marlin, the sailfish, the
tarpon. After all, the *Sea Wynn* had the flying bridge, the
crow's nest, boat tanks, the works. But Ed would never
budge. Maybe it was in part because of what had happened
when he first bought the *Sea Wynn.*

Around the pubs of Long Island, where seafaring mates
would gather for a bit of grog and a chanty or two, legend
had it that the *Sea Wynn* was haunted, doomed to stay in
its mooring as long as men sailed the seven seas. Ed never
moved the yacht because it never occurred to him or to
anyone else to ask whether or not it had a motor. All Ed
saw was a gleaming white boat! The previous owner, who
must have had the IQ of a snowflake, forgot to tell him
that he had leased his yacht to the government (actually
the Coast Guard) for the duration of the war for one dollar
a year—a very patriotic thing to do. The Coast Guard saw
no reason to have all that horsepower going to waste, just
sailing people up and down our rock-bound coast, so they
removed its Rolls-Royce engine. How it was done I don't
know, but then explain the ships in the bottles to me! I
guess it was a sort of maritime hysterectomy.

After the hostilities the boat was returned to its mooring.
Its patriotic owner was rewarded with a medal and an
autographed picture of Cesar Romero, whereupon he sold
the boat to Ed, happy to get on with it, as he was by this

time a ski buff. He got a very fair deal and an autographed picture of Ed to put up beside the one of Cesar Romero.

During all this no one thought to open the hatch. All Ed was interested in was where he was going to hang the Japanese lanterns. So the boat lay there in her mooring for two years, and during the summer months a proud and happy Ed would invite the cast from his show to be his guests and join him on the fantail for some tall ones. All was well until one night a former admiral in search of the head opened the hatch and saw the gaping maw. The apoplectic Navy person roared out the news.

So here we were on the *Sea Wynn* that first morning with her motor grudgingly reinstalled, fishing for little porgies. Most of the boats in these shallow waters where we fished were powered by outboard motors and were named after the master's mates . . . *The Elsie*—Bensonhurst, *The Selma*—City Island, *The Blanche*—Hoboken. There were also several fishing barges in the vicinity with fifty or sixty disciples of Isaac Newton aboard.

The *Sea Wynn* would float into this flotilla of Archie Bunkers with her brand-new engines churning, her whistles blowing, and her huge anchor being dropped, all of which chased any hovering fish to quieter waters. Ralph and John and, of course, Earl ("Tailor to the Stars") would emerge in their idea of the proper attire for fishing. They wore little brimmed hats adorned with hand-tied flies and lures, waders on their feet, and each one carried a creel. The fact that there weren't any rainbow trout within two thousand miles of Denver did not deter these anglers, who blithely attempted to flycast off the stern. Finally Ed made his entrance. Our polished host sashayed onto the deck wearing an elegant black cashmere robe tied with a gold tasseled cord, a white silk ascot, and a captain's hat adorning his bald head to protect it from the sun. In his right hand was a can of worms he had bought from a man on the dock, and in his left hand was a fragile fishing rod right out of Woolworth's window. His guests were aghast as he dropped his already baited hook over the side and waited. He looked as if he had as much right to fish as Mother Theresa running Elizabeth Arden's.

I had already observed that Ed did everything in life as though it were a piece of stage business. He would see an object, react to it with a large take, rest his head on his chin in contemplation of it, then he would realize what it was—a chair, perhaps—and make a big show of sitting down. His little battered fishing rod pitted against his guests' brand-new Abercrombie and Fitch gear might have seemed laughable, but he had used it many times before, and in record time he caught three beauties, did another giant take, and lisped to us as he ambled back to his cabin, "Well, that's enough for lunch!"

The sail was beautiful. The sun and the air and the sea were intoxicating. Keenan and I were so exhilarated that we tramped around the boat playing *Mutiny on the Bounty* with a lot of shouting of "Mr. Christians" and "Captain Blighs," dressing up and playing pirate, dancing around the deck, falling off the railing into the water, and generally making complete nuisances of ourselves. Ed was very patient, but later on that first day, after he had had a sip of his evening cocktail, he shook his head and, pointing a finger at us, he said, "You know what you two cutups are? You're yacht comics . . . only funny on a yacht!"

On the day Ed did his "Fire Chief" broadcast, I used to go over to the theatre and sit with him through those three long hours between shows. (No tape then. They did the show live at eight P.M. for the East, then live again at eleven for the West.) That's when we really became friends. His advice and help were invaluable. I realized that Ed as the "Fire Chief," a.k.a. "The Perfect Fool," and Ed Wynn who became my surrogate father were two completely different characters. One never interfered with the other. Ed knew exactly who he was and loved every minute of it.

I found that this was true of many stars, for example Edgar Bergen, whose show I later did. I used to do various characters on it, including a bumbling, blustery business tycoon who laughed at his own jokes and later developed into Mr. Magoo. He was a great foil for Charlie McCarthy. In my four years on that show, I never once heard Edgar as Charlie fluff a word. On the other hand, Edgar—as Edgar—had a hell of a time, stumbling over the simplest of lines! Some of the funniest bits were Charlie's ad libs over Bergen's boo-boos. Bergen as Bergen couldn't ad-lib a belch at a Hungarian dinner.* Bergen as Charlie made idiots out of John Barrymore, W. C. Fields, and Tallulah Bankhead, to name just a few of the guest stars.

The same is true in my case with Mr. Magoo. In my thirty-six years—and who knows how many chuckling, double-talk lines later—I have to the best of my knowledge never, as Mr. Magoo, made one goof. But as Jim Backus? Who's counting? The same is true of Thurston Howell of *Gilligan's Island*, né Hubert Updyke III of radio. I have followed the comedy greats on many, many benefits, from Bob Hope to Milton Berle to Danny Thomas on up and down, and at tumbrel time I have learned in the interests of self-preservation to keep Jim Backus out of it! If I walk out and do a few lines as Mr. Magoo, by the time the audience has stopped laughing, I am long since out the door and gone.

I learned a lot from Ed. If I got an offer of a job, I would take the script to Ed and he would read it, we would discuss it, and then read a scene or two aloud. The hardest thing to learn is how and why to turn down a part, especially while living in a five-dollar-a-week room. Ed once asked me point-blank, "Do you want to be an actor or a star personality?"

That's a tough one to handle. I thought it over for a while. "I guess I want to be a star personality. But I want

*Courtesy of Fred Allen.

to build it with something of substance, something to be proud of."

"Then you have to settle for one character—one character with which to be identified. Take me, for example, or better still, take Fred Allen. He plays a character called Fred Allen, and that's all he plays. He lets the cast dazzle the audience. But he's the pivot, the star.

"I've seen you kidding around, Jim, and you do two characters I like . . . the one you did for me the other night— the rich boy, sounds like F. D. R.—and that other one you fool around with, the one that bumbles around and chuckles. Pick one and concentrate on it. Keep the other in your hip pocket in case the first one doesn't work out. Look at Jack Benny. He developed that character people think is really Jack. But far from it! He lies back and gets the laughs and the money. Gracie Allen, that's a great character she has! The list goes on and on. In most cases the cast can act circles around the star."

And believe me, he was right.

"So, young Mr. Barrymore, get out of here and skeedaddle over to Earl Benham's. Get Earl to make you a suit."

An Earl Benham suit! I couldn't believe my ears.

"Maybe now," Ed added, "you'll look like a star."

During those weekly three-hour "Fire Chief" visits I learned more about acting, producing, and comedy writing than I could have in any college. Ed was a fascinating man who knew that he was part of a fast-vanishing era, an era where giants walked the earth . . . Babe Ruth, Bobby Jones, Jack Dempsey, Bill Tilden, Jimmy Walker. It has been called the "Era of Magnificent Nonsense"—"Pyles Bunyon Derby" (a race), Floyd Collins, who was trapped in a cave and had the entire country's fascinated attention for almost a year, Balto the Wonder Dog, who carried the serum to Nome and wound up playing thirty-nine weeks at the Palace.

Ed was a witty man, very fast with the ad libs. A number of years ago, when he was quite old, we were at a party when a slightly mulled freeloader came over and entered into our conversation. At one point he said to Ed, "You probably knew Mark Twain." Ed thought for a moment. "I don't even know Hal Holbrook!" As he watched the intoxicated gentleman leave, he turned to me and said, "There goes a man who staggers to a different drummer!"

Politically, Ed was slightly to the right of Attila the Hun, but during the actors' strike there he was, walking the picket line even though he was a producer.

Ed loved the ladies, and when he was out on the town, he always had two long-stemmed beauties, one on each arm. Unfortunately, his marriages didn't work out. How many? We don't remember. (When Henny and I started this book, we agreed to write as we remembered, not to make it a compilation of numbers.) I remember on that first cruise on the *Sea Wynn*, he announced that he was getting married again to a beautiful girl. The skipper of the boat congratulated him. "Here! Here!" he said. "Mr. Wynn, I'll plan a lovely two-week cruise, little hideaway islands, where you can skinny-dip by the—"

Ed interrupted. "That's very nice of you, Captain, but just twice around the harbor will be plenty."

"On your honeymoon?"

"Skipper, at my age all that happens is just a little dust comes out."

I lost touch with my surrogate father, not that I hadn't read about him; Ed Wynn was a pretty tough guy to lose track of. I saw pictures of him—same jaunty little hat, not the same long-stemmed beauties on his arm, though. He later confided that George Jessel, self-appointed eulogist to the Hollywood stars, and Ed's long-time nemesis, seemed to have the pick of the crop.

Keenan told me his old man asked for me—he wanted to see his favorite yacht comic. Ed had sold the *Sea Wynn*. "Not to that eulogist George Jessel," he added, a twinkle in his eye. Keenan also confided that Ed had been suffering from Parkinson's Disease for some time, which explained the constant nodding of his head. He suffered in silence. Only his close friends knew about it.

This Is Henny . . .

By now Jim and I had moved to Hollywood. It was 1946, and he was working constantly, going from one picture to another, plus sucking the last drop of blood from that dying medium, radio. Then Ed joined the hegira to the Coast. He bought a lovely house in beautiful old Brentwood Park. He kept what we now call a low profile—only an occasional lunch at the now-renowned Hillcrest Country Club "Round Table," where the wit was supplied by Groucho Marx, Milton Berle, Eddie Cantor, Jack Benny, Danny Thomas, and, of course, George Burns . . . and, unfortunately for Ed, that celebrated eulogist George Jessel.

Suddenly everything Ed touched turned sour. He tried doing a nightclub act in Las Vegas, but the audience of gimlet-eyed hoods and their siliconed doxies were not the kind that appreciated his fey and clownlike humor.

He then did what few performers of his stature would do at that time, *The Ed Wynn Show* on that capricious infant, television. As with early motion pictures, most actors of distinction would not touch TV. Naturally, he won the award, the first of its kind—a brand-new award called the Emmy.

The celebration was held at the Ambassador Hotel that first year, and Ed, in his acceptance speech, innocently made the biggest boo-boo possible by telling the TV audience of hundreds that the committee had informed him two weeks in advance that he had won. Naturally they did! Obviously they had to! Why else would he show up for this obscure award? Before the great day somebody called Jim and asked him to be a presenter. "We had a very short meeting of the entire committee," the voice informed Jimmy. "It took no time to decide. It was unanimous. Jim Backus to present the award to Ed—Jim and nobody else but Jim!" Jimmy was sorry to tell him that he was doing a new movie and leaving that day for location. Without missing a beat, the voice asked, "Do you have Mickey Rooney's phone number?"

Ed retired once again to the fastness of Brentwood Park. He surfaced from time to time, but from the world of show business he had retired.

This Is Jim . . .

One lovely afternoon, Easter Sunday 1956 to be exact, we assembled in Jose Ferrer's den to read our parts and discuss them before starting to shoot his new movie, *The Great Man*. Joe was to direct as well as act in it. This was a provocative tale about a super TV star, loosely based on a certain shit-kicking, hypocritical luminary. I asked Al Morgan, who wrote it, if this far from flattering portrait of the red-haired, ukelele-playing bullshit artist was really Arthur Godfrey. He looked me square in the eye, the lying bastard, and said, "No, it's based on Pat Boone." Actually, it was an olio of all the demagogues with their pitchman's approach to the Bible ("Send in the money and get your own monogrammed snake!"). Those charlatans with their "Aw, shucks," and "Jiminy Cricket" charm controlled the afternoon airwaves.

In the screen play the Great Man has died, and his network has decreed a week of mourning with an open-coffin catafalque in the rotunda of a TV theatre. Joe Ferrer played a network newsman who interviewed the people as they shuffled by the bier. Henny played a role that Hedda Hopper, among other reviewers, said should have gotten her a nomination for the Oscar. She was a Bronx housewife who came to the Great Man's weekly show only because of the samples of coffee, hand lotion, and chicken soup they gave away. It was hilarious! As Joe with his microphone talked to the fans, the audience began to realize that the man in the coffin was really a monster. I played his secretary/press agent/stooge, whom he kept around to do his dirty work by threatening to expose him as the hopeless alcoholic he was. I had one scene with Ferrer in which he gives me a drink to stop the shakes, while I recount my hideous years with the Great Man. I'm very proud of that scene. And I might add that Jose Ferrer is one hell of a director. The entire cast was talented and professional and a joy to work with. The movie was a prestige picture that, for example, played one art house in New York for more than a year. It has now become a "cult film." (I mistrust anyone who calls a movie a "film" or refers to a book as a "great read.")

That Sunday afternoon is etched in my mind. There we were at Joe's house, the girls in their pretty Easter dresses, each of us listening intently while we took turns reading our parts. There was an empty chair next to Joe. I wondered who was missing, when suddenly in the doorway there was Ed Wynn, looking splendid, complete with a boutonniere on the lapel of his formal morning suit. He lisped a few hellos. Joe rose and greeted him and said to the assembled cast, "I've saved the best for the last. In this scene, hopefully to be played by Mr. Ed Wynn, it is a mom and pop radio station, and Ed, as the owner, tells how he had taken in the Great Man and not only given him a job, but had brought him into his home, where he and his wife treated him like a son. Then one day they took a trip, leaving the radio station in the Great Man's care. On their return they found him gone, the liquor cabinet rifled, and the radio station completely ravaged. Not only that, but the townspeople said that he had spewed obscenities over the airwaves."

This was to be told by Ed in monologue fashion—no cuts—just Ed relating page after page of dialogue without a break in the film. This meant he had to be word perfect for the shot to succeed. As Joe recounted what he intended to do with the scene, I watched Ed pale, then his head started to go and his hands shook.

"Now," said Joe, "I've asked Mr. Wynn to do his scene, so we may all get the feel of the entire story. Any time, Mr. Wynn."

Ed excused himself for a moment, taking Keenan, who played the part of a money-grabbing promoter, and me with him into the next room. "Boys," he whispered, visibly shaken, "I can't do this! What does he want me to do—audition? Me? One of the great comic artists of our time?!" As he talked, his broad "Fire Chief" lisp sneaked in. "Does Mr. Ferrer know that I was the first comedian to play his home town, Puerto Rico—"

Keenan broke in. "Look, Dad, everyone knows how great you were, but this is a part! A real part! You've got to put the Fire Chief away. This is a whole different ball game."

"But," said Ed, "I've never read a straight line in my life!"

"I know that, Dad, but you've got to go out in that room and show Joe and the cast that you *can* read a straight line—that you can act!"

Ed looked around for something to hold on to. He grabbed me. "Jim," he said weakly, "you're my friend. What do you think?"

"Mr. Wynn, I know you can do it! Just go out there and show them!" (I guess I was no longer a yacht comic.)

He shot me a look, pulled himself together, and, as he strode back into the den, I heard him mumble, "I wasn't this nervous when I followed Jolson at the Winter Garden."

Ed's reading was great. When *The Great Man* opened, and wherever it played, he got a standing ovation.

Ed next did *Requiem for a Heavyweight* on live television—live, mind you!—which was on the air *before* the release of *The Great Man* and in which this talented gentleman, now well into his sixties, was so brilliant. A whole new career opened up for him. It was crowned a little later by his performance in *The Diary of Anne Frank*, for which he received an Oscar nomination.

* * *

As I sit here in my den now, I keep glancing at a picture on the wall. It's a photo of Ed's seventieth birthday party at Chasen's. Surrounding him are Sharley and Keenan Wynn, Georgia and Red Skelton, Paul and Peg Stewart, Rosemary Clooney and Jose Ferrer, and Henny and myself.

Just one more word about Ed. Two years later, on his deathbed, he looked up at Keenan and said, "One thing, Keenan."

"Anything, Dad. I promise."

"Don't get Jessel."

Chapter One—
The Beginning

March 10, 1941, was really chapter one, page one, of my life. That was the day I met Henny.

It was a raw, blustery day. I had about eight cents in my pocket, and I was about to be locked out of my room at the Piccadilly Hotel. Out of desperation, I went to see my agent, Herman Levin, who was trying to raise some money to produce the show in which he had promised me a part. Hermie was confined to bed with a strange virus probably brought on by malnutrition. He lived a couple of blocks away from me at the Hotel Royalton in exquisite squalor.

He didn't have any encouraging news for me, and as we sat there commiserating with each other, there was a knock on the door. I instinctively leaped up and headed for the closet. In those days a knock on the door meant only one thing—the credit manager.

"Take it easy," Hermie said. "It's probably just the nice doll from upstairs who promised to bring me some soup."

So I said, "Listen, do you mind if I climb into bed with you, Herm? I could do with a little soup myself."

"Don't be a jerk," he replied. "I'll leave you some. Answer the door and be nice to her, Jimmy, she's got a hot plate."

I opened the door and there she stood, her arms out-stretched, a vision of loveliness, holding a bowl of clam chowder. There was only one jarring note. She was wearing a pair of overalls and was covered from head to toe with plaster. She handed me the bowl and, in a voice that sent shivers up and down my spine, said, "Here's the soup." Then she disappeared down the hall in a cloud of plaster dust.

I turned to Hermie and said, "That's the sexiest-looking bricklayer I ever saw."

"Bricklayer?" he replied. "Oh, you mean the plaster. She's a sculptress. Her name is Henriette Kaye, and she acts, too. She's also a pretty successful model. That's why she's got so much soup up there."

What's the use of kidding? I was smitten, though I never believed it could happen. It was a case of love at first sight. So I coerced Hermie into letting me return the soup bowl. A little while later I timidly knocked on her door. She opened it, revealing the most amazing sight. For here in this old midtown hotel Henny had created an attractive studio. The walls were Wedgwood blue and covered with paintings. One wall was book-lined, and there were pieces of white sculpture here and there. There was a record player going and, best of all, she had a real fireplace with a big log blazing away. All this for seventy dollars a month rent. This lovely plaster-covered creature ushered me into a big easy chair and said the three loveliest words in the English language, "Have a drink?"

I, in my best Noel Coward drawing-room manner, re-plied, "If you don't mind, I'll have a short beer."

She went directly to the phone and called the nearby delicatessen and, in a voice of authority, said, "Please send up six bottles of chilled Schlitz." My cup was running over. Here was a girl with a lovely face, a divine figure, and, best of all, she had credit.

We had a wonderful time in front of the fire talking about this and that while I artfully concealed the hole in my shoe. This enchanted evening came to an end all too soon and this bewitching creature, with whom I was now madly in love, bade me good night at the door. I took my last look at her, silhouetted in the light from the dying embers. Then she slipped something cold into my hand. It was the last bottle of beer.

"Here," she whispered into my ear. "Take it home and drink it in bed."

This Is Henny . . .

When you swung down the street carrying your hatbox, everybody knew you were a model. There was never a hat in that box, just your changing smock, a hairbrush, some makeup, a mirror, and perhaps a book or two. Nobody knew how the hatbox thing got started. Why did all the New York models carry their gear in hatboxes? Why not suitcases, briefcases, anything? But it was our trademark, and we reveled in it. We loved the business of being photographers' models. Nowadays the girls who pose have one big advantage. They move. They don't just stand there. The cameras in the thirties were too slow for that. We had to hold the pose endlessly, or so it seemed. Steichen was my favorite. He would set everything up, do a slight rehearsal, arrange the lights, and then scoot down in front of the camera under the lens to talk you in. I understand that's the way the great director George Cukor worked. It was fun! Steichen got a thousand dollars a shot . . . unheard-of in those days. He gave me a hundred! Unbelievable! We only got ten dollars from *Vogue*.

Ah, but *Vogue* was like working for the Theatre Guild on Broadway, which I had done in the past. The Guild paid everyone but the stars Actors Equity minimum: twenty-five dollars a week if you were a junior member and forty if you were a senior. I was a senior, having been a member of Equity since I was a baby. But it was the prestigious Theatre Guild! It helped your career even if your show was a flop. The show that I did a few years back, *Chrysalis*, bombed. The stars were Humphrey Bogart, Margaret Sullavan, June Walker, Elisha Cooke, Jr., and that glorious actor, Osgood Perkins, Tony's father. They each got sixty-five dollars a week!

It didn't matter much to me that we folded. I was loaded. Although I was primarily an actress, I got a hundred dollars for modeling three mornings a week for illustrator Russell Patterson, another hundred-and-a-quarter a week from Warner Brothers East Coast for doing an occasional bit and posing for a lot of cheesecake. Then there was that hundred bucks from Steichen once a month, and all I could pick up in my spare time. Also, I was beginning to get commissions for my sculpture, which I had been working toward all my life.

What energy we had! None of this dough ever saw the inside of a bank. Broadway was a small community. We all knew each other and helped each other. I spent my money wildly. I picked up tabs, gave parties, gave presents, and lent it to my out-of-work actor friends, who certainly would have done the same thing for me. I carried a sack full of cash for sudden emergencies—a dime for two doughnuts and coffee, a nickel to call an agent, taxi money for a sudden possible job. And, more often than not, a sizable sum to bail out a colleague whose hotel had changed his lock and was keeping his trunk. There was a lot of that. The Belvedere still has Bing Crosby's trunk in its storeroom. The Piccadilly had Jim's, so he asked me for help, and then he had a better idea—so I moved him into my studio at the Royalton. We lived like that for two years and, when we were sure, we got married. All at the wonderful Royalton! What a hotel!

This Is Jim . . .

After a few simple formalities—such as Henny paying my back rent to bail my trunk out of the Piccadilly Hotel, and getting my shoes half-soled—I moved into her studio, and two years later we got married. We spent several blissful years there. Ah, the Royalton! What a hotel it was then!

Located at 44 West Forty-fourth Street, right across from the more famous Algonquin, the Royalton was full of very interesting residents at that time. Most of them were actors, some of them rather famous, along with some writers. Among the latter were Robert Benchley—who was much beloved by the staff and everyone who lived in the hotel—and the not-so-beloved critic George Jean Nathan. Down in the lobby sat a young man named Tennessee Williams, who was writing a play on hotel stationery. Practically everyone who lived there was either a writer, an actor, a playwright, a producer, a ballerina, or a director. The lobby was fascinating, and every evening we all hung out there.

The Royalton had no restaurant, no room service, and no bar. Its main entrance was on Forty-fourth Street but, because the hotel was very long and narrow, there was another entrance directly opposite it on Forty-third Street. It was a very skinny lobby one block long. On the left, and directly in the center, was a long hotel desk, plus a cage for the cashier and a screen that partially hid Ruthie, the lone telephone operator. Directly across from the desk was an elevator with two doors that opened and closed with a clang, and the elevator rose with an asthmatic whine. We also had a stairwell that ran the hotel's full six stories. The lobby, of course, boasted those requisite shabby but comfortable big, dull gray sofas and club chairs, and those hideous standing ashtrays with the bottoms full of sand that would lean any way you wanted them to.

Red, the night clerk, was behind the desk, smiling a welcome from dusk to dawn—Red and his bottle. He was a plump, sweet-faced, balding, redheaded man who spent his nights watching over his charges and nipping from his bottle. Then he would go home to his apartment in Brooklyn, which he shared with his mother, a huge Swedish masseuse who would knead all the poisons out of his body so he'd be free that night to start the whole cycle all over again.

On my first night as a resident of the Royalton, a tarty-looking woman sprinted from the Forty-fourth Street door and then raced through the lobby. Without slowing down as she passed Red, she simultaneously winked at him and threw him a dollar. She fairly leaped out of the Forty-third Street door and was gone from view.

"Oh, oh," said Red. "Here comes either the first of the night or the last of the day." I was fascinated.

Then a young woman with badly bleached hair ran into the lobby, winked at Red, threw down her dollar, and scooted out of the Forty-third Street side. A few minutes later a gigantic Texan, complete with Stetson hat and the yellow rose of Texas in his lapel, stomped in. Irate at being bilked by his lady companion, he weaved around the place and chose Ed Wynn, who happened to be visiting Robert Benchley at the time, as his target.

The Texan began to bellow, "To hell with it! To hell with all of you! To hell with this fleabag! It's probably full of Jews and cockroaches anyway!"

Ed tensed.

"You a Jew?" continued the Texan.

"No," said Ed as he started for the elevator. "I'm a cockroach."

Charlie, the bellboy, doubled as the night elevator boy. He lived down in the cellar with his cats. Charlie wasn't exactly a boy, as he had celebrated his seventieth birthday. He wore an ancient uniform and always had at least one sleeping cat draped over his shoulder. "Your stole just winked at me," Henny once told him.

Every morning the elevator door would open and unload a dapper little bantam cock of a man, who would stride pompously over to the desk, and the following dialogue would take place:

"Good morning, Mr. Riley." Red would smile. "Trust you slept well. How are you, Your Honor?"

Mr. Riley was a well-known judge who had once run for governor of New York opposite Franklin Delano Roosevelt.

Mr. Riley ignored Red's query and held out his hand. Red reached under the desk and brought up a glass of water, in which lay submerged a full set of dentures. Without a word, Mr. Riley would take them out, slip them into his mouth, and strut out of the hotel.

Every night I saw a very altered and plastered Mr. Riley. This impeccably dressed little judge would, in the evening, be wearing old gray pants, sneakers, a shirt with no tie, and an enormous, ancient, long gray sweater. He would carry a flashlight, and there was a long string around his neck with a large whistle hanging from it. Mr. Riley also was obviously not wearing his dentures, which he had left in the custody of Red. He would stagger determinedly down the Royalton steps, holding his flashlight aloft, and park himself directly in front of the Algonquin bar. With the whistle in his mouth and the flashlight aloft, he proceeded to direct traffic. Cars came to a screeching halt. They tried to back out. They did everything but move in the right direction. After the large after-theatre traffic had been completely snarled, the neighborhood cop would ride up on his horse. New York's finest knew exactly with whom he was dealing and always patiently said, "That was very nice, Your Honor. But why don't you go inside to the bar and have a drink? Let us take over for you for a little while, huh?"

Mr. Riley would spin around, accept his praise, and reel into the Algonquin bar while the policeman started his task of untangling the traffic.

My years with Henny at the Royalton . . . what a time! I had married a very resourceful woman, and I learned exactly how resourceful soon after I moved in with her.

After a hard day of trudging the streets looking for work,

I would come back to the charming studio to be greeted by my darling lady, and after a few correctly chilled martinis, she would serve me a delicious dinner before the fireplace. I couldn't figure out where the cooked food came from since, as I said, there was no room service and no restaurant in the hotel. But I wasn't about to ask any questions. I never had it so good, and I wasn't going to upset the applecart. There was always a great variety, too. Every night there was a different casserole, a different salad, and a different dessert. I kind of wondered why we never had steak or chops, and one day when I timidly requested a hamburger, I discovered that Henny had a secret. She had our hotel bathroom all rigged.

In a curtained wooden crate under the sink she had pots, pans, canned goods, and condiments. On another dolled-up crate full of dishes, linens, and silver, there reposed her one-burner hot plate. Using only packaged, frozen, and canned foods (since there were no garbage facilities and no cooking allowed in the rooms), and with the timing of a DiMaggio, she cooked our meals. All paper cartons were burned in the fireplace, even in summer. The cans were smuggled out by a well-bribed bellboy, the garbage was flushed down the best disposal unit of them all, and the dishes were taken into the shower with us. Her refrigerator was the wide bathroom windowsill, and while we were eating, the electric coffeepot was gurgling away. Even after we finally moved into an apartment with a real stove and a full kitchen, she still used only one burner for the better part of a year.

Ah, Henny and the Royalton . . . my two great, colorful ladies!

New York Radio

It was funny, the devious and meandering turns my career took. In other professions the course is either upward or downward, with some kind of form, but not so in our business. As you know, I started out to be a serious legitimate actor. However, as you also know, the Depression was then in full swing. It was next to impossible for a newcomer to get anywhere at all in the thirties since even the established stars and well-known players were featuring cardboards in the soles of their shoes. In my case, the yen to eat overcame any artistic urge, so along with countless other actors, I decided to try radio again, this time not as an announcer but as an actor. Once again my friend Garson Kanin came to the rescue. He knew a director who was holding auditions for a part in a daytime serial, and he managed to get me an audition.

As I stepped into the NBC elevator the next morning, I caught a glimpse of my friend, aspiring actor Gregory Peck, then a page escorting a tour group through the facilities. The elevator rose and stopped smoothly. The doors silently opened on the renowned third floor. At the far end was a reception desk, and beyond that a very long hall with eight radio studios, four on each side. Benches ran along the walls from the elevators to the reception desk. They were full of actors and actresses. This time I would get past the guard at the desk. I had a pass!

I walked along the hall past those actors, all of whom had some pages of script they were going over. Beside the desk, along the side hall, was a row of telephones that were never idle. The moment an actor came off the air, he went to the phone to check with his "radio exchange" to find out where and when his next show was. I wondered if I would ever be so lucky.

I got the part, and before I knew it I was doing twenty to twenty-five shows a week! When you realize that for a soap opera, for example, there was only an hour rehearsal, then on the air for fifteen minutes, and the big prime-time shows only took two hours to rehearse, you can see how that was possible. The big shows had to be done twice, however, as there was no such thing as tape. So, as you know, we did it live for the East and then again three hours later for the West. When you figure that the daytime shows paid thirty-five dollars apiece, that I averaged three a day, and that I usually topped off the day with a big show like *Gangbusters*, *Henry Aldrich*, *The Fred Allen Show*, or *The Kate Smith Show*, which paid about a hundred bucks a throw—plus spot announcements, commercials, and hitchhikes,* I was doing all right! In addition to this, after I married Henny, with her modeling, acting, and sculpting, she too was earning her share of the loot, and using her salary to keep the stockholders of Saks Fifth Avenue very happy!

I still wanted to be a serious actor, but I felt that I had to compromise. The compromise, I must admit, lasted quite a few years. In the back of my mind I was sure that I would return to the theatre when I had a few bucks in the bank

---

*Hitchhike: A Madison Avenue term for an added commercial tagged onto the end of the show, usually plugging one of the sponsor's subsidiary products. These paid eleven dollars and took five minutes of our time.

and when *that part* came along. Now mind you, that money we actors were making in radio was before the big tax bite, and we had no agents' fees. It never occurred to us at the time how good we had it. Just think, we had no lines to learn, no costume changes to make, no costume expenses, no press agent or fan mail burdens. We got no recognition. All we got was money.

There were about fifty New York actors and actresses who had radio all sewed up. They got all the parts. Fortunately, I became one of them. During my "Actors Anonymous" days, one of the dullest parts I had the pleasure of playing was that of Dick Grosvenor, Stella Dallas's son-in-law. After I got to Hollywood, I discovered that five other actors had played the part before me, namely, Everett Sloane, Barry Sullivan, MacDonald Carey, Frank Lovejoy, and Richard Widmark.

One day I got a routine call for a job that I didn't realize was going to change the entire course of my life. It came from Perry Lafferty, vice president of CBS—and later NBC—but at that time a young radio director fresh out of Yale. He said he was doing a Damon Runyon series, and this week's show was the story of a group of gangsters who were trying to "fix" a football game between the "Harvards" and the "Yales."

"Thought you would be able to play the captain of the Harvard football team," he said. "It's a cultured guy. Hell, you could do it with your eyes shut!" Even then Perry was full of boola boola! So I got the rehearsal time and hung up.

I told Henny about it, and she said, "Why don't you play it like the rich guy you do at parties? You know, that imitation you do right before you put the lampshade on your head and I have to call a cab."

"Aw, c'mon," I exploded, "that's strictly parlor stuff. I can't do that on the air!"

"Look," she said, "you're going to play a Harvard man, and they all sound like that! Any Harvard man I ever went out with sounded like he was born with a silver spoon in his mouth and they forgot to take it out."

So to keep the peace I did it her way. I could have killed her! No one paid any attention to what I was doing except the band. They laughed. In our business, when the band laughs it's usually the kiss of death. Musicians have an offbeat sense of humor and laugh only at "inside" jokes. So I decided never to do that character again.

Strangely enough, just one week later I got a call to play an advertising executive. At this time, a young Canadian named Alan Young flashed on the radio scene as a summer replacement for Eddie Cantor. The executive, as originally written, was to appear on Alan's show and give pompous criticisms and belittle the star. After an all-night argument with Henny, I again tried THAT CHARACTER. This time I struck a nerve. The next week the advertising man I was playing became the rival for the affections of Alan's girl. The following week he was made the richest man in the world and given a name—and Hubert Updyke III began to emerge. The jokes given me were wonderful and still are. The writers just loved to write Hubert. After all, just think, a man who has all the money in the world! Everyone has, at one time or another, wondered how it would be to be that loaded!

We gave Hubert an indulgent father whom he referred to as "Dear Old Dad," thousands of Cadillacs, and a mansion in what he called "Booverly Hools." The wonderful thing was that despite all his wealth, Hubert was lovable. He wanted to be liked but, in trying to endear himself to people, he made the mistake of bragging about his wealth and position. It was a perfect combination. Alan Young played a mild, timid schnook, and Hubert intimidated him with his blustering, bombastic, pompous statements. It must have been a success, because we got countless letters from mothers and teachers begging us to get off the air as the kids were starting to talk like Hubert!

Hubert was beautifully written and constantly won awards

for the Best Supporting Character. It went on for a long time, and you can still make his acquaintance, as later he became the character on *Gilligan's Island* called Thurston Howell.

Hubert's love for a dollar overcame any sex drive he might have had. Here is a typical love scene:

HUBERT: Ooooh! You are such a nice girl, I think I shall take you for a ride in my Cadillac station wagon. It will be so romantic. We'll listen to the music of Guy Lombardo and his Royal Canoodians.

GIRL: Oh, have you a radio in your car?

HUBERT: No, I have Guy Lombardo and his Royal Canoodians in my car.

Or the switch:

HUBERT: Oh, I do love to put my little pink body in the bathtub and, while I'm taking a bath, I just love to listen to the music of the New York Philharmonic Symphony.

GIRL: Oh, you have a record player in your bathroom?

HUBERT: No, I have the New York Philharmonic in my bathroom—and that trombone player has such a cold slide!

Or:

HUBERT: Ooooh! I like you. I'm going to give you a pearl necklace from my own private oyster beds. Each pearl will be the size of a watermelon.

GIRL: Why, that's silly, Hubert. How can little oysters make pearls the size of watermelons?

HUBERT: We use whips!

When asked why his estate in Beverly Hills was so clean, he said, "I have a sign on my roof that says: 'Pigeons flying over, please fly upside down!' "

HUBERT: My estate in Booverly Hools is not only the biggest, but it's air-conditioned.

ALAN YOUNG: So what? Lots of people have houses that are air-conditioned.

HUBERT: On the outside?

Looking back, I realize Hubert and Thurston have been very good to me. After not believing in the character and fighting Henny all the way, in the final analysis it was Hubert who brought me to Hollywood. Alan's show caught on, and he got a movie contract, so the entire radio show was brought to the Coast on January 6, 1946, to emanate from Los Angeles.

On the other hand, I often wonder if Hubert didn't do me dirt. One day, after we had gotten the tickets to California (but not too late to back out), I got a call from my then fairly obscure playwright/director friend, Garson Kanin. He said he had written a little play and wondered if I would be interested in playing the lead. I said, "Gar, you must be nuts! I've got my big chance to go to Hollywood!"

So Gar said, "Go, Jim, and God bless you. Grab the loot and sit in the sun. Besides, my play will probably be a flop anyway."

The name of the flop? *Born Yesterday*!

TRADITION!
(An Invitation)

Traditions have vanished from old Tinsel Town
no more can you dine in a derby that's brown
every major's been sold to some corporate putz
and the Coconut Grove long ago lost it's nuts.
Gone are the bars where the famous once drank
The Garden of Allah's turned into a bank
although Chasen's remains and is still making money
Dave has departed and Maude isn't funny.
What the moguls once did is now done by committee
and the backlot at Fox is now Century City

But be of good cheer in this time of transition
we still have one single surviving tradition
when each New Year's Eve, in their home in Bel Air,
there's the Backus's annual year-end affair.
It's always a star-studded, gala occasion
with your hosts, Jim and Henny, and lots of libation.
The revelry starts thirty minutes past seven
then custom decrees that it stop at eleven.
That's the time Jim and Henny lock up the wine,
so you're free to go elsewhere and sing Auld Lang Syne.

To miss this soiree would be worse than sedition
it's more than a holiday bash, it's tradition!

R. S. V. P.   472-6781   Black tie

(Written by John Aylesworth)

Our annual welcoming
sign! *(Nate Cutler)*

Michael Caine and Henny

Cesar Romero, Jim, and Greer Garson—1977

Jim, Danny Kaye, Hedda
Hopper, producer Perry
Lafferty, and Henny—1967

Henny and Sidney
Sheldon *(Nate Cutler)*

Henny, Jim, and Phyllis Diller—1972 *(Yani Begakis)*

"We kiss a lot in Lotus Land." George Burns and Jim—1987 *(Nate Cutler)*

Zsa Zsa Gabor and Jim

Carroll O'Connor and Henny

Henny and Richard Burton

Keenan Wynn and Jim *(by Nate Cutler)*

Fernando Lamas, Henny, and Esther Williams—Lamas approves

Groucho and Henny

George Burns, Fred MacMurray, June Haver, Henny, and Cesar Romero—1987
(Nate Cutler)

Jim and Danny Thomas with Barry Jacobs at the piano—1986 *(Nate Cutler)*

Hooray for Hollywood

On January 5, 1946, I sat in the club car of the *Santa Fe Chief*, its lonesome wheels wailing as it made its way through western Arizona ready to plunge into California. My mind kept racing in tempo with its wheels. Was it smart to drop everything I had built to take a chance on that ephemeral bitch, Hollywood? Three hundred dollars a week, great! But what if the show bombs and isn't renewed? Alan Young? How can he miss? A juvenile who's funny? Me? That was a whole different ball of wax.

I could have made a screen test before we decided to leave New York, but Al Altman, the MGM talent scout, informed me that first I would have to have a nose job, electrolysis to thin out my eyebrows, and, it goes without saying, a whole mouthful of caps. The only thing they understood in Hollywood was beauty. Man created in the image of Robert Taylor and Tyrone Power!

Ty Power, I said to myself, come to think of it, he still owes me that ninety cents dinner money. Who am I kidding? I wanted to go to Hollywood more than anything else in the world. How I envied Henny in our compartment sleeping like a baby. A real frontier lady, a born gambler! Makes a bet and goes with it all the way! Suddenly I had

a terrible thought. What if *Born Yesterday* is a hit? I rein-
forced myself by finishing my nightcap and gave the waiter
a dollar. After all, I can afford it. I'm sure to run into Ty
Power at Ciro's or the Macombo.

I remember the ride from the little Pasadena depot ("railroad station to the stars") to the Beverly Hills Hotel that
morning so many years ago. Henny had been here before
as a starlet, so this was a refresher course for her, and she
loved California. The city of Los Angeles, she always felt,
was her spiritual home. What impressed me most was the
clear, pure air and the incredible brightness of the sun. It
didn't shine, it sparkled!

Our driver took us through the scenic route, the Los Feliz
section where the silent movie stars once lived. Then up
Hollywood Boulevard. Hollywood and Vine—those crossroads made famous by Bob Hope in his radio monologues.
Grauman's Chinese, where parts of the stars were immor-
talized in cement—Lassie's paws, Mae West's breasts, Clark
Gable's ears, and, of course, Betty Grable's legs. Then over
to Sunset Boulevard, the beginning of the Strip. "Oh, look,
Henny! There's Schwab's Drugstore, where Lana Turner
was discovered!" I must admit, it was tough not to gawk.
I had to maintain my New York theatre snobbery even
with Henny. The "Hollywood-is-great-if-you-happen-to-be-
an-orange" syndrome!

"Oh, look, Henny! Look, there's the Château Marmont,
home of Greta Garbo!" I couldn't help it.

So this was Hollywood. I had no preconceived notions
about it. To me it was a place where all good actors went
if they paid attention and stayed relatively sober. What
fascinated me, in addition to the clean, sweet-smelling air
and the shimmering sunshine as we drove up the Strip,
was the elfin-sized snow-white buildings that housed the
offices of agents, public relations people, advertising agen-
cies, and the like.

I remember later that week having an appointment at
the offices of the ad agency, J. Walter Thompson. The name

itself gives one goose pimples. They wanted to see me about doing a commercial. "How do I get there?" I asked, thinking of course that it, too, was somewhere on the Strip.

"Simple," I was told. "We're in Hollywood, slightly south of the 'Tail of the Cock,' across from Selma Avenue. Go into the Thrifty Drugstore and walk all the way to the back, up the stairs to the second floor, and there you are." J. Walter Thompson? Over the Thrifty Drugstore? That's like going to Rome and finding the Vatican over a pizzeria! But this was still an uncomputerized world, and there wasn't much need for a West Coast office, if indeed that's what this really was. Actually, it was more like a mail drop.

That first morning I checked my Omega. I realized that we had been on the road for an hour. That was fine with me. I was busily checking the landmarks on the Strip. Ciro's, Macombo, Elmer's, The Troc, and, right near Doheny at the end of the Strip, The Cock and Bull—the hangout for the English set—where you could get a hell of a Melton mowberry pie.*

Not much farther up Sunset was the small, pink Beverly Hills Hotel. I looked around the lobby. All our worldly possessions in three hand trunks, Henny's lucky carpetbag, two tin makeup cases, a string-tied cardboard carton, and a tub of Henny's clay were sitting in the midst of a sea of Vuitton luggage. As George Gobel so aptly put it, "I felt like the world was a tuxedo and I was a pair of brown shoes."

The lobby was jammed. Unable to find a place to live, and with hotel accommodations long since depleted, some of the people who couldn't get rooms were sound asleep in the chairs and sofas, and one was out like a light on top of a steamer trunk. At that time, there just was no available housing. Nothing new was being built as yet, and every soldier who had passed through Hollywood and had gone

---

*Melton mowberry pie: An oleo of meat and potatoes in a cement crust.

to the Stage Door Canteen and danced with Rita Hayworth had come back here to stay. We were fortunate in that *The Alan Young Show* was under the aegis of advertising agency Young and Rubicam, the head of which was married to Loretta Young, who, with Irene Dunne, owned the Beverly Hills Hotel. Since Young and Rubicam was the agency for General Electric, our sponsors, that explains why Henny and I and the rest of the cast were ensconced there, permitted to live in the Beverly Hills Hotel for six days— Then out! To where? Not only that, but we had no transportation. There were no new automobiles to be had, just used cars. Good ones were hard to find and exorbitant. The used-car business was booming, but not for us. We didn't have the capital. It was all cash under the table. Everything was expensive. We had enough money to eat on, but gingerly. Ordering was strictly from the right side of the menu.

It was the cabs that were killing us. We had to use them to find another place to live. Most of them were manned by young veterans who were out here for one reason only, to become movie stars! They drove cabs part-time so that they could afford to look for acting jobs.

As luck would have it, on one of my fifteen-dollar-one-way jaunts to NBC, my driver, a big, good-looking kid, asked me why I was going there. I told him I was on my way to do *The Eddie Cantor Show*, then I explained that I was from radio and the Broadway theatre. He was so impressed, I didn't have to show him my diploma! Then he asked me if I could help him with a scene he was to do for Warner Brothers. He pulled over to the curb and handed me a script. We both got out and worked on the scene. The kid was so grateful he never dropped the flag. The trip was on him. Then word got around and I helped out several of his colleagues, so our transportation problem was greatly alleviated, and I had founded the first drive-in drama school!

We were terrified by the prospect of being literally thrown

into the streets. Finally, after wining and dining total strangers, having mysterious meetings, and handing out a case of impossible-to-get Scotch, we got a room. Quarters at the brand new Bel Air Hotel. And, best of all, we could stay for three whole weeks!

The Bel Air Hotel, as it stands today, is one of the most beautiful spots in the country. It is hard to believe, but the main building was once a riding stable. When we checked in, the hotel was only half built and not too far removed from its origin. They had barely taken the horses out! Here we were, at an exorbitant forty dollars a day, our room half completed—no heat, no hot water, no mirrors, no chest of drawers, no room service, and no bar! Just a bed, a lamp, and a mirrorless bathroom. We had no car, and the nearest eating place was ten miles away by taxi. We had enough money, but we nearly starved to death. There we were, in one of the wealthiest communities in the world, surrounded by mansions, living in a stable! All we needed was the three wise men to come over the hills in their Cadillacs.

This Is Henny . . .

Almost every day Jim took his usual taxi ride to NBC, CBS, or ABC to do one show or another, as he was not limited contractually to *The Alan Young Show*, while I was deep in a taxi scouring the town for another place to live. No luck! Los Angeles was really packed. Everybody was here. Show business was at an all-time high. The town was full of actors. During the war, due to the shortage of actors, the studio signed whomever they could. Now, with the war over, the boys had come back from service to pick up their old contracts. In 1946, due to the entertainment boom, the list of performers under contract to a major studio was about the size of the telephone book of Ashtabula, Ohio.

One evening, when our three weeks in the world's most

expensive barn was almost up, I could hardly wait for Jim to come home from work. "Jimmy!" I shouted exuberantly. "Guess what! I found us a place to live!"

The next morning, as Jim and I drove up to our new house, I felt like the Wandering Jew, and I was not too sure about Jimmy.

This Is Jimmy . . .

The place that was to be our new home looked like the house at the opening of any Dashiell Hammett movie. The kind that starts (italics), "It was nineteen thirty-two. . . . Things were really rough. . . . I moved to California. . . . I'd gotten a job selling insurance. . . . I walked down that shabby palm-lined street, eighteen cents jingling in my worn gabardine suit. . . . I turned up the walk. . . . Rang the doorbell. . . . And there she stood (*music stab*). She was wearing a pair of mules and a coffee-stained kimono which was slightly open . . . from her chin to her knees. . . . I knew then I would have to murder her husband (*music chord*)."

As I looked at this house, I knew that I'd have to murder my wife. I have never seen such a place. It was a pink stucco igloo, all of twenty by thirty, but the walls were four feet thick. Instead of windows it had slits, obviously designed for pouring boiling water on peddlers. Growing out of the center of this strange abode was a sixty-foot palm tree that seemed to be suffering from some scrofulous disease.

The cabdriver carried our bags, the carton, and the tub of clay over to the moat, and Henny opened the nail-studded door with a slime-covered key. Then I saw the inside. Let me tell you, it was a shock to the nervous system. What a switch! In contrast to the bastard Moorish exterior, the inside was entirely blue glass and chromium, the worst sort of modernistic. With a flick of the key, architecturally speaking, we had skipped seven generations. The floors were covered with dun-colored wall-to-wall carpeting, and I'm not too sure I should have left off the g. One room leaked into the other. The living room dissolved into the dining room; the dining room slopped over into the kitchen; the kitchen drooled into the pantry. Sort of the "anklebone's-connected-to-the-shinbone, the-shinbone's-connected-to-the-knee-bone, the-knee-bone's-connected-to-the-thighbone" school of architecture! The bedroom was enough to set sex back fifty years. What passed for a bed looked like a big, square red toupee. There was no such thing as a direct light. The whole thing glowed like Captain Nemo's *Nautilus*. It looked like the interior of a flying saucer.

After we had explored and Henny had unpacked and parked her tub of clay, I felt kind of ashamed of myself. After all, it was better than the streets. Anyway, it was only temporary. In a month or so we would find ourselves a nice place in Beverly Hills.

Two years later we found it. There were no tears in our eyes as we closed the door and turned the lock on our first home and pointed the prow of our brand-new 1934 Packard into the setting sun to Beverly Hills.

Rocks on the Roof

This Is Henny . . .

We had rented a house on Linda Crest Drive that was to be "home" for the next eight years. We took it on a month-to-month basis so that when we had saved enough money for our yet-to-be-found dream house, we could get out fast. We paid $350 a month, unfurnished. The eight years of rent we ended up paying came to $33,600, which would in those days have made a nice down payment on Blair House.

They tell me the trend today is for split-level houses. Our new rental was way ahead of its time. Each of its nine rooms had a level of its own. It stood on a half acre of ground, all of it vertical. Linda Crest Drive is a short street off Coldwater Canyon in the hilly section of Beverly Hills. Coldwater Canyon itself is a mountain pass to the San Fernando Valley. Our street branched off this north-south mountain and was on an offshoot mountain going east-west. The house, which was on the north side of the street, was on a hill of its own. So we were living on a hill that slanted in three different directions. To put it simply, to get to our house, you went up Coldwater Canyon till your nose bled, and then you turned right. In front of our house was a rolling lawn, all of it straight up. The garage was a cave dug out of the left side of this lawn. It was directly on the curb of the street with no sidewalk and no driveway. You drove off the road into the garage at a steep and tilted left. This took a bit of practice! To show you how really steep the whole arrangement was, the steps to the front door wound around and around right over the roof of the garage! We later found out that the life expectancy of a child living in this house was, with luck, three days. There wasn't one single child in any part of that neighborhood. At trick-or-treat time I was stuck with a lot of chicken corn and candied apples, as not even the bravest little delinquent could reach us!

This Is Jim . . .

The house had nine rooms and four baths. Each room was on a slightly different level. On the first plateau there was a porch and a vestibule that led to a dropped living room, and I do mean dropped. Below that was a dropped dining room, then a dropped kitchen and a pantry. Around the corner, and I hope you are winding with me, was a dropped maid's room with its own dropped bath. Starting with the vestibule again, to the left of that and down were our bedroom and Henny's dressing room and bath. Then my study and bath, which were three steps up around the corner. Down from my digs was a den with an inside barbecue pit and a Dutch door that I hated. I would always forget to check and see if both parts of the door were attached, and I would invariably rush through to be knocked flat on my back by the half that stayed shut.

Outside of the den through that Dutch door was a split-level garden with many wild and beautiful rosebushes. As you walked along the narrow brick path with its great thorny bushes lining either side, and down many little twisting stairways, you came to a playroom, which was directly below the living room. There was no way to get to the playroom except through the garden path and those steps. A very practical arrangement for parties. Around the corner from the playroom and down another flight of stairs was a beautifully equipped laundry. Still farther along and down two more steps was a storeroom, and around the corner from that, almost at street level, was an open area under the porch that looked like another garage. Since there was no way into that "garage" except through the garden, we used it for the storing of logs.

From a housekeeper's standpoint, this house was far from ideal, since the soiled clothes had to be taken through the narrow-pathed, rosebushed, steep-stepped, curving, winding-back lane to the laundry. We never had much luck with laundresses. Not one ever came back for a return engagement. And as for dragging the garbage, the bottles and cans and the assorted trash to the street curb for pickup, one took the same route three twists lower.

A friend of mine who has his own place used to fly over our house regularly. When I asked him why, he said that our place and the surrounding terrain made him nostalgic for his years in the Second World War when he was flying the "Hump."

We moved in in March, and it wasn't until later that we discovered that our house was a good twenty degrees hotter than any other house in Beverly Hills. We were in a hole, in a canyon completely surrounded by mountains. The air just drifted in and stayed. It stayed until the rains came and cleared things out a bit.

Four hundred feet up on our left lived Ginger Rogers. Four hundred feet up on our right lived Leopold Stokowski. Directly in front of us, straight up on a sheer cliff, perched the home of Jascha Heifetz. Our neighbors were within yodeling distance.

Another lovely advantage of living in our house-in-a-hole was the fact that when television appeared on the scene, none of us in that entire area could get any reception whatsoever. George Raft, who lived on the corner, bitterly resented not being able to get the fights and the ball games. He hired a live-in engineer to solve his problem. For months we lived in hope, pricing television sets. Day after day we watched as the engineer erected on the roof of George's southern colonial mansion a tall, hideous metal structure. It was very impressive. Passers-by thought that Raft's house was a small radar station. George gave all the neighbors permission to hook on, and things looked so promising that we bought a beautiful television set. When the great day came, nothing happened. Nothing! Not even in Raft's house. Not even in Raft's house when we were all ordered to hook off! He saw absolutely nothing! No picture. No test pattern. Not even any sound. A few weeks later Mr. Raft moved away to better reception, taking his Eiffel Tower with him.

We tried again and again, but it was not until four years later that we got television reception. Louis Calhern, another neighbor, brought a man to see us in the dead of night. This man laid great illegal coaxial cable from a master antenna on the peak of a mountain two miles away at the cost to each neighbor of four dollars a foot. Our phone bill shot up because we all had to check with each other and decide which station to look at, as all of us on the cable had to shift at the same time. One dissenter and we all wound up with Scotch plaid.

This Is Henny . . .

While we lived in the Linda Crest house there were many strange happenings. We had one fire, one explosion, one robbery, and an epidemic of rocks on the roof. Now I must explain that on the right side of the house there was a tangled jungle as far as the eye could see, but on the left —or laundry side—we were separated from our next-door neighbors by only the four-foot width of that backyard lane. Fortunately, theirs was a Moorish house with three-foot-thick walls, or it never would have survived. This house was owned by Fred and Daisy Seeburg, two very kind and patient neighbors. Mr. Seeburg was an avid stamp collector whose den was on a level with our laundry room. The laundry contained the boiler and the heating system, which we never understood. Each room was individually heated by four little buttons: low, medium, high, and off. That's all we ever had to do, press a button. But every time we pressed one it caused the pilot light to shoot clear across the garden path right into Mr. Seeburg's study, singeing his Mozambique Purples. After that happened several times, it was gently called to our attention. Our landlord replied to our complaint by sending a heating expert, a Mr. Rudebega, who spent the entire day fixing it and assured us that all was well. From that time on the heat worked fine, except that every time we pressed a button the whole house would shake and from the boiler room would come a low, ominous rumble. One night when I was out, Jimmy pushed the heat button and the whole thing exploded. It knocked him into another room and blew Mr. Seeburg's stamp collection almost into orbit.

There was another mysterious occurrence in our Beverly Hills house. I was awakened almost nightly by the sound of very loud snoring, which we took to be sleep sounds emanating from the family next door. When we got to know them better, we discovered that they slept on the other side of their house. We finally decided that it was Jim's snoring ricocheting off the mountains and let it go at that. Then one day, after a heavy rainfall, we found large, barefoot, muddy footprints leading from the laundry all the way along to the garden path to the street. The mystery was further heightened when our latest laundress came running upstairs to tell us there was a ring around the laundry tub, as though someone had taken a bath. Two clean sheets had been used for towels, and an empty bottle of Manischewitz Extra Dry was lying on the ironing board. Could it be that we had a guest? We called the police, who shrugged the whole thing off with, "Oh, it's only that guy again. Don't worry about him. He's harmless. He's an itinerant gardener who works around these hills, and when he's had one too many he'll sleep anywhere. Just tell your laundress to keep this door locked and he won't bother you anymore." We weren't too terrified because the fact that we never caught him proved that he was a light sleeper. The ring around the tub proved that he was clean, and the empty Manischewitz bottle testified that he believed in gracious living. Anyway, we locked the laundry.

This Is Jim . . .

One beautiful Sunday a short time later, Henny and I were at the golf club about to tee off when we got a message to call our telephone exchange. The message was very cryptic. It said, "Go home. Your house is on fire!" We rushed home from the golf club to find our little slanty street jammed with bystanders, police, L.A. County's Sheriff Biscauluiz on his white horse, firemen and all their fancy new fire-fighting equipment. The fire was out. Actually, the fire had been quite a serious one. Smoke had seeped all through the house. It seems that Mr. Seeburg, our good neighbor, had been watering his cactus on the laundry side when he spied flames shooting out of the cave where we kept our logs. He turned the hose on it while his wife called the fire department. The fire chief, after investigating with his ax, took us aside and made his report. "Mr. Backus, upon investigating, we found some empty wine bottles. The only thing we can figure out is that someone must have fallen asleep on your logs with a lighted cigarette. I'm afraid I'll have to report this to the police, as the zoning laws clearly state that it is illegal to sublet any portion of your house without first appearing before the real estate board."

Henny and I like to believe that our fire was started not intentionally, but that our nonpaying tenant, who obviously liked al fresco dining, had laced his crepes suzette with too much Manischewitz and the whole thing had gotten out of control. I will say one thing about him, though, he was awfully quiet. We never heard him go in or out. He was clean, and he never entertained girls in his room!

This Is Henny . . .

The strangest thing by far that happened to us during our Beverly Hills tenancy, and continued throughout the entire eight years, was the epidemic of rocks on the roof. I mean this literally. For eight years, off and on, the roof of our house was bombarded by rocks of all sizes. In the annals of the Los Angeles Police Department, if they keep annals, this is down in the books as an unsolved mystery. And believe me, the Los Angeles Police Department did everything in its power to solve it.

We hadn't been in the house two full weeks when the first rock struck. It wasn't too late at night. We were just sitting around when all of a sudden something hit our roof with a dull thud that literally jarred the house. We shrugged it off as some new form of California living, but those thuds continued throughout the night. We were a little puzzled but finally concluded that it was coconuts or avocados dropping from the trees. The following morning I found rocks, some of them actually broken, all around the house. The average one was the size of my fist. Naturally we called the police. They assured us that it must be the prank of some high-spirited kids necking up in the mountain.

No more rocks were thrown for a time. Then it would start up again, and again, and maybe only one rock would be hurled. Or it might just continue for an hour or two, or again throughout the night. Then peace would reign and we would be lulled into a false sense of security. Then, at three o'clock in the morning during a particularly violent rainstorm, one especially large boulder came thumping down. It was just as though whoever was throwing them was trying to find out if we were paying attention. Occasionally he varied our rock diet with a bottle or a log, and once two flashlight batteries tied together with wire landed with a crash.

This Is Jim . . .

At first the police didn't take this too seriously, but later, when one of the rocks bounced off our shale roof onto Mr. Seeburg's hand-tiled roof, causing about four hundred dollars' worth of damage, they really closed in. They tried everything. Whoever it was who was catapulting the missiles at our roof was able to see exactly what was going on. It was eerie! He would cease firing at the first sign of a police car and, five minutes after the cops took off, he would lob one rock, no more and no less, at us, as if to say, "Don't get smart with me!"

There was no logic in any of those attacks. Henny began to believe the house was haunted. Our friends thought we were out of our minds, as our assailant never attacked when we had company. However, one night Keenan Wynn and his wife were over and they were busy explaining how the whole rock episode was a product of our imagination, when, pow! Believe me, they were dumbfounded. This so intrigued Keenan that he organized his motorcycle brigade into a posse which for weeks went tearing through the hills.

The police were still trying to solve the case. They stationed two special officers in jungle garb in the bushes outside our house. The rocks continued, but they were never able to find their source. Mr. Seeburg and I worked nightly with the police. We tried to figure out approximately where the rocks came from. We took a baseball player from the Dodgers' team up to the top of the hill nearest the house and had him throw a few samples. Even when the wind was with him, he couldn't come within a hundred and fifty yards of our roof. They had to come from directly above—and there was nothing directly above. They next went on the theory that maybe someone was strapped to a high tree. They stationed men around every high tree in the vicinity, and still it continued. Finally, though, they thought they had it solved. They figured there was only one way it could be done. They decided that whoever it was had devised a giant slingshot.

One day they called in great excitement. "Congratulations," they said. "We just solved your case! We just caught a man way over in Woodland Hills who has a slingshot made out of old inner tubes and he's been doing the same stunt with rocks over there."

As soon as the police hung up, our sniper gave us three fast ones, as if he could almost hear our conversation. After a while the police lost interest, and Henny and I got quite used to our rocks. As she put it, "I think we've had rocks on our roof in some shape or form ever since we've been married!"

This Is Henny . . .

P.S.:

Two or three years ago I was meeting Jim at a cocktail party at the home of Kathy and Darren McGavin, which was almost directly across the street from our old house with the rocks. As I was getting out of my car, I spied Merv Griffin parking his and I ran up to him. "Merv," I cried. "Right over there is the house you make me tell about every time I'm on your show, the one with the rocks on the roof!"

"Where? Where?" he called.

So, taking him by the hand, I led him up that curvy, windy, slanty street, and there it was. And there was a big "For Sale by the County" sign that read, "This house is possessed. . . ." Boy, was it ever! We doubled up with laughter.

"Merv, listen, please tell Jim and Darren about the sign,

and I'll run home and get my camera. I can't let this go by, so I'll be at the party a little later."

I flew home to Bel Air, which is a good thirty-five minutes each way at that time of day. By the time I got back it was too dark to get a picture, and when I went back the next day the sign was gone.

Our house was possessed! You bet it was—and it obviously still is, as every six months or so there is the same sign out front:

> FOR SALE—
> THIS HOUSE IS POSSESSED
> BY THE COUNTY

Hello Bubbie

It was a crystal-clear morning, with a tang in the air and a bite that made living in California a joy. Drag out that thesaurus, whip up those metaphores, and you will still come up short. If a man can have ten mornings like this in a lifetime, he's ahead of the game. As I crossed the ridge of the hills, there it was, Cahuenga Pass, the San Fernando Valley against a sky of pure cobalt blue. Smog? That was something crackpots talked about, nonsense like the Lock Ness monster or the Yeti.

I drove into the voluptuous Valley to Barham Boulevard. Soon I would have a glimpse of Warner Brothers Studio, my home for the next month. My first part in a movie! How did that come about? Pure luck.

We were doing our own radio show, *The Jim Backus Show*, and someone in the audience from Warner Brothers saw me, liked me, my agent moved in for the kill, and here I was, about to start work in an unpretentious little comedy called *One Last Fling*. It was to be shot in twenty-one days—revolutionary then! It had a good cast: Alexis Smith; Zachary Scott; Ann Doran, who later played my wife in *Rebel Without a Cause*, and me.

So there I was, driving along in a spanking new red Ford

convertible that I had just purchased from a dealer known to us all as the Thief of Burbank . . . aptly named, I might add. To my left was the Lakeside Country Club, home base for Bing Crosby and Bob Hope. And past that, could that be Taluka Lake? That's a lake? It was only about two hundred yards long and fifty yards wide. I had assumed after reading so much about it that it would be a real lake, like the one back home.

Warner Brothers Studio! I saluted the guard. With a wave of his clipboard he admitted me into the studio, and the dream of a lifetime began to come true.

There were things that Jack Warner couldn't abide. He had to personally check them out. Was the tie okay? Did the makeup man remember to include the inside of the ears? Had the body lady done the hands? I spent two days being costume tested from head to toe. I passed muster. My choices of ties were okay, my ears checked out. My hands were dark enough. Mr. Warner saw every foot of my tests. A far cry from the "wham-bam, thank you, ma'am" of today. He did, however, insist that my black, bushy eyebrows had to go. So they removed some and bleached the rest. Then they gave me a crew cut and, so it shouldn't be a total loss, they bleached my hair.

Like my first day in school, this morning in makeup was forever etched in my memory. The makeup department was in a separate building. It consisted of a string of cubicles, each one presided over by a makeup artist. Dominating these tiny rooms were old-fashioned barber chairs. The walls were covered with bulb-studded mirrors. There was also one enormous room about the size of a basketball court with many more barber chairs, and makeup tables the length of the walls. This room was for the extras and bit players. When I arrived at six A.M., the big room was already full of people milling around, shouting, joking and smoking, while munching away on the inevitable doughnuts and swilling cups of java.

I stopped at the door and gave the attendant my name.

He rapidly scanned his clipboard. "Oh, Jim Backus." He smiled. "You're in *One Last Fling*. Your room is number thirty-eight, right across the hall. Lee Britton will be your makeup man on the picture . . ." (as indeed he was, intermittently, for the next twenty years).

I was greeted at the entrance to cell thirty-eight by a good-natured bear of a man with an infectious laugh and a blaring voice. He sat me down in the barber chair and said, "I wangled it so you're the only one I do on this show." (Old-timers always refer to the picture they're doing as "the show.") He then stuck his head out of the cubicle and shouted, "Crullers and coffee for Mr. Backus! On the double!" He turned to me. "Now, I know you're new." He lowered his voice to a conspiratorial whisper. "First picture, right? So let me give you the lowdown. Unless you keep on top, these characters will walk all over you. Watch out for the first assistant—he'll try to get you here as early as possible. Less worry for him that way." The boy arrived with the coffee. "It's about time, Junior. Next time I want you to be standing here—coffee in one hand, cruller in the other."

"You shouldn't have done that," I told him.

"Oh, yes, I should," he said. "Now drink your coffee."

"Shouldn't you be making me up?"

Lee winked. "Hell, no! I'll make you up in the trailer on the set. That way you can grab a little shut-eye," he said protectively. "I'll have a chat with the assistant and have him change your call to seven forty-five. That's plenty of time. That way you can have coffee and Danish in your own trailer. Here, let me turn your chair around so you can get a better view of the snake pit. Everything here is by the numbers. Just like the army, only more so."

The big room across the hall was filling up, as were the cubicles. The noise was deafening, and the room was redolent of greasepaint, spirit gum, and more smoke. At this point, in through the bazaar came the featured players on their way to their cubicles. The arrival time you could get away with was in direct ratio to your salary, which also determined whether you got your own coffee and doughnut or whether it was brought to you by one of the gofers. Your salary also determined whether you had a portable dressing room on the set, your own assigned parking space, a trailer outside, and how close it was to the sound stage. And, oh, yes, the telephone. Anyone whose salary was under fifteen hundred a week had to go out of the set and stand in line at one of the public phone booths. The caste system was as rigid as the one in India.

The stars and featured players who were actually *under contract* to Warner Brothers had permanent dressing rooms, more like little apartments. They were situated past head makeup man Perc Westmore's office, but they usually stopped in the big room to spread an all-purpose "Hi, there."

The first star to arrive was Errol Flynn, early morning vodka in hand. "Cheers!" Everyone loved Errol. "In like Flynn!" they shouted back. Next to arrive was Ida Lupino, who spotted her stand-in and her wardrobe lady. "Morning, loves," she called in her lovely voice and English accent. They rose and kissed and giggled off. Next came one of the most imitated actors in the world, Humphrey Bogart, who growled a grouchy, perfunctory "Morning" to the huddled masses. "Morning, Mr. Bogart," they muttered and went back to their coffee. A pleasant "Good morning, Ronnie" brought a cheery "Well, hi!" from Mr. Reagan. Weaving in and out of the room were several harassed young men. They were the second assistants, whose job it was to herd the people belonging to their "show" out of there and onto the sound stage, so that when the first assistant roared, "Places, please! We're on a bell!" the cast would be in place.

I finished my coffee, rose, and started to swivel my chair back to its original position. Lee was gathering up his makeup to take to the set when all hell broke loose. In came a parade—a makeup man, a hairdresser, a script clerk, a personal maid, two men in Italian silk suits who had to be agents, and a studio publicity man, whom I recognized. In the middle of this mélange was the queen of the lot, larger than life, her hair done up in bright, flashing curlers, clad in a billowing, wildly colored caftan, chattering away, laughing, and twirling her cigarette . . . Miss Bette Davis! Her co-workers looked up and grinned. It was plain to see that they adored her. This morning they had worked out a gag. When she shouted her stylized "Good morning," they—in unison, twirling their cigarettes— answered in kind. Realizing it was a joke, she shouted back a most regal "Bless you, my children," and went off screeching good-natured obscenities, curlers flashing, cigarette blazing, looking for all the world like a demented Chinese dragon.

I was still sitting in my trailer, fully made up, waiting for at least a rehearsal before they called lunch. Twelve forty-five. I nervously went back to studying my script— and wishing this first day were over with—when the door opened and a cheery voice said, "Well, well, if it isn't Mr. Backus from Cleveland. Good luck, Mr. Backus." It was my good friend and star of the radio show *Big Town*—and fellow alumnus from the American Academy—Edward G. Robinson. "Hi, Eddie!" I was thrilled.

"Shun," he said, before disappearing into the blazing sunlight, "don't try to drive the *Twentieth Century Limited* on a teaspoon full of coal!" I laughed as he left. What a dear man he was!

The second assistant stuck his head in the door. "Rehearsal. First team. Places!"

I wasn't nervous anymore.

This Is Henny . . .

Jim has always been a free-lance actor, which means that even in the golden days of Hollywood he was not under contract to any one studio. When he finished a picture, he was out of work, with all the insecurities that go with being unemployed in any other business. After a couple of weeks of unemployment, he is always, even today, literally out of his mind. It's not unusual, believe me. I recall one night just a few years ago, when Henry Fonda, a close friend and neighbor, dropped by on his way home from work for a quick drink. I mixed him a welcoming bourbon and soda. He took a large gulp and looked up at me. "We finished the picture," he said sadly.

"So?" I asked.

"That's it," he said glumly. "I'll never work again. They'll never call me for another part. *They've had Fonda!*"

This from one of our great actors and certainly a huge star!

"Oh, Hank," I laughed, "not you, too! That's awful, that attitude from you of all people!"

"Oh, yeah!" said Hank defensively. "You think I'm bad, you ought to see Jimmy Stewart!"

This Is Jim . . .

Well, somehow, despite my negative mood, my agent would finally call. He never under any circumstances said, "I know you need a job, so let's go out to Twentieth Century-Fox and see So-and-So. I think I can get you a part in his picture." Instead, it was always on a casual and social basis like, "Sweetie (agent talk), if you've got nothing better to do and don't feel like playing golf, let's drive out to Twentieth and have a chat with one of the boys. It's a nice day and I want to show you my new Cadillac. I'll pick you up in, say, half an hour. Oh, and incidentally, before I get there, get a crew cut, take your glasses with the heavy frames, wear a button-down shirt with a bow tie, that tweed sports jacket, the gray flannel slacks, and whatever you do, don't wear those alligator loafers!"

After decoding this Hollywood phone call telling me what to wear, I knew I was up for the part of a college professor. My agent knew it, and what's more, the "boy" we were going out to have a chat with knew it, but for any of us to admit it would be breaking some strange Hollywood gentleman's agreement.

As soon as we reached the studio, we were ushered into the producer's office. After the introductions, the producer asked us to be seated. He paid no attention to me from that moment on. He and my agent kept up a running conversation of chitchat. They discussed everything under the sun except the business at hand. Ten minutes later, when we were out in the street, I broke the sound barrier. "Well, Al, how did it go?!"

"You got the job," he answered. "You start on the fifth, twenty-five-hundred a week, with a four-week guarantee."

How the deal was consummated was—and still is to this very day—a complete mystery. Al and the producer never once mentioned me, the part, or the money. I was sitting right in that room every minute, and all I can think of is that they must have had signals like a tobacco auctioneer.

Father Was a Fullback was to be shot at Twentieth Century-Fox and on location at the Coliseum for the football sequences. In the cast were Fred MacMurray, Maureen O'Hara, Thelma Ritter, Rudy Vallee, talented little Natalie Wood, and me. What pleased me most was that it was to be directed by Elliott Nugent, who had written and starred in *The Male Animal*, the quintessential college play.

The first day of shooting was on the New England street on the back lot. It was an after-church scene, so everybody worked, the full cast. They had one of those giant crane cameras on a boom, and in the first shot it was to zoom down and pick up all the houses along the street. Then it was to come in on me in front of my house, where I was to say hello to my next-door neighbors Fred MacMurray and his family, Maureen O'Hara and Natalie Wood, as they approached. Then a tight shot of all of us as they watched me making a mole trap in my front yard. We did it in one long take.

After that take, our director, Elliott Nugent, seemed to be having difficulty explaining to the cameraman how he wanted his next shot. What they were arguing about was a close-up of me. Mr. Nugent wanted to back up the camera and then zoom in tight for my close-up. The argument got hot and heavy. Finally, while he was shouting at the cameraman, he forced the makeup man to put a full makeup on him and, at the same time—to further prove his point—he borrowed my wardrobe sweater and got into my position on the lawn. Then he borrowed my glasses and indicated that I should sit in the director's seat on the crane. The next thing I knew I was zooming forty feet into the air on a seat no larger than a catcher's mitt—and without my glasses! I couldn't see a thing! I knew this was irregular, but I realized from my vantage point that Elliott Nugent, on the ground, looked so right in my part as the professor that I assumed he was going to fire me and replace me with himself!

I could hear the argument still raging down on the studio street, and, from what I could make out through the blur, there was a lot of scuffling and traded punches. Then cars started to arrive, and I heard the voice of our producer, Freddy Kholmer, joining in the altercation. Then Dick Sales, who wrote the movie, then the voice of the first assistant director—but they shut him up fast. If you weren't making at least fifteen hundred dollars a week, you were not allowed in an argument.

Suddenly a covy of Cadillacs appeared, and out stepped Darryl Zanuck, looking like an irate chipmunk, flanked by his associates. Finally, someone noticed me hysterically screaming for help from my perch. And that was when Darryl Zanuck lowered the boom on both of us. Mr. Nugent was fired on the spot, and I was sent home.

I was a very confused actor. What did I do? Was it my fault? After all, that was my scene they were shooting when all hell broke loose. But what was it all about? What hap-

pened? As I drove into our driveway, there was Henny. She
was doing her urgent "phone call" pantomime.

She waved me into the house and onto the phone. It was
Al. "Sweetie, baby (agent talk), good news! The picture is
shut down. And Elliott Nugent is going to the hospital
with a nervous breakdown."

"Is that good news, Al?"

"Wait, lover, you haven't heard the best part. They're
going to take it from the top with another director, and
it'll take them four or five weeks to find one!"

"Okay, Al, but what's good about that?"

"Sweetie," he assured me, "all you have to do is sit around
and wait. Play golf ... anything you want to do ...
make love to Henny under a table at Ciro's. You're on full
salary!"

What happened was they did shut down for five weeks.
They finally got a new director, a formidable man named
John Stahl, who at one time actually had his own studio.
He was one of the founding fathers of cinema and had
directed and produced some of the really big T and S
pictures.*

John Stahl was a drab and humorless gray man who had
gray hair, wore gray suits, gray shoes, and a gray homburg,
which he never took off. I never saw him without his hat
or heard the sound of his voice. He gave us our directions
through an assistant, which is unheard of. At one point I
did a very long and complicated scene in only one take. I
deserved and expected some sort of reaction from him—
maybe not an "*Olé*," maybe not the tail and the ears,
but at least a nod. All I got was a shrug and the words,
"Print it!" Whereupon he left and disappeared into the gray
fog. He was truly Mr. Congeniality. This dour European,
I thought, was the last man on earth to direct a comedy

*T and S: Tit and Sand. Movies with a Biblical background, lots of
desert scenes and, if you were lucky, Shelley Winters, topless.

about American football and college high jinks. The only person on the set he showed any affection for was that irrepressible little girl, Natalie Wood.

Natalie, at the age of eight or so, had the acting skill of a Duse. She was the most adorable child I have ever seen. She could dance, sing, do dialects, anything! She was the cutest little lady in pictures, and what's more, she knew it! She was also a born flirt, and she reduced Mr. Stahl to a tower of strudel. She was forever leaping into his lap, twining flowers through his hair, and hugging and kissing him. The fact that she could sing folk songs and chatter away in Russian was too much for his middle European heart.

But I was wrong about John Stahl. He must have known what he was doing. *Father Was a Fullback* was a winner!

The phone rang. A voice said, "Hey, bubbie!" It was Al, my agent. "I'm on the phone right here in my new Caddy. How about that?!"

I was dazzled. "How *about* that," I answered weakly.

"How are you, sweetie?" he asked.

"Fine. Thanks to you and that five weeks off with pay. I feel great. Played some golf while I was off."

"Hope you didn't get too much sun!" Al sounded alarmed. "If you have a good tan, it means you're out of work. Nobody wants you if you haven't been working. Watch it! Stay pale till you get established."

"What about Cary Grant? Oh, I get it. He's established."

"Listen, Jimbo," he continued. "Why don't I pick you up in half an hour. We'll have lunch at Musso Frank's— oldest restaurant in Hollywood. Those writers like F. Scott Fitzgerald, William Faulkner, and Zane Grey used to eat there. Great place!"

"A sort of hangout for the literati, eh?"

"Them, too," he assured me. "And while we're in the neighborhood, we'll drop in at RKO—cutest little lot you ever saw. Gotta go now, my other phone's ringing. Ha! Ha! That's a joke, boy!"

Two hours later we were walking along Hollywood Boulevard on our way to that "cute little lot." It was the only one in town that Al couldn't drive on. They barely had room for their stars.

"Let me tell you about Howard Hughes," said Al. "He bought RKO sight unseen. Then at three o'clock one morning he decided to go and see what he had bought. He had a hell of a time convincing the guard at the gate to let him in. How could a tall, skinny guy in tennis shoes who had just parked a beat-up 1937 Chevy at the curb own a movie studio—and at three o'clock in the morning, yet! Well, he somehow convinced the guard and got in. He walked around, stuck his head into a few stages, cased some open offices and wrote a note, which he left with the guard. All the note said was, PAINT IT!" I laughed. "That's a famous story. True, too!" Al assured me.

"Will Hughes be at whatever we're going to this afternoon?"

"No, he's probably at his office."

"Then he's on the lot?"

"No, no. His office isn't at RKO."

"Why not?"

"Nobody knows why not. It's on the Goldwyn lot. I guess 'cause he's a man of mystery."

"I give up, Al. We're beginning to sound like Abbott and Costello."

"He's a great guy to do business with."

"Who?"

"Hughes. 'He's on first.' " We both laughed. "Listen, you want to hear a story?" He didn't wait for my answer. "You know the Roland Petit Ballet?" I assured him that I did. "Believe it or not, they're clients of mine. Well, Hughes caught them at the Hollywood Bowl. Two of the ladies are amply endowed. He's a 'jug man.' "

"I know," I said. "I've heard that story about him designing the famous cantilevered brassiere."

"Anyway, those boobs and the mesh tights drove him nuts, so right away I get a personal call from him, direct —none of that crap with the secretary. I think he was calling from a pay phone, I could hear the clang. Anyway, he tells me to be on the corner of Dayton and Rodeo, right near my office, in fifteen minutes, and he'll pick me up. So he picks me up in that beat-up old Chevy and he starts to drive. We go up Benedict Canyon clear to Mulholland, then way up to the top. Then he stops. He parks the car, he turns to me, and he says, 'How much?' I tell you, Jim, selling a ballet company doesn't happen every day. Anyway, I stayed calm. I wrote him out a number, pretty hefty, too. He looks at the number, doesn't bat an eye, nods, and says, 'It's a deal.' Then he writes me out a check for fifty thousand dollars, sort of a down payment. You gotta admit that's better than a handshake. He doesn't shake hands, anyway. Germs."

"That's weird!" I volunteered.

"Sure is. A 1937 Chevy? The least he could do is get himself a nice new Caddy."

I didn't see much of the "cute little lot." Al hustled me into the office of a producer named Bob Sparks. Seated there in proper pecking order were a director, a cameraman, a production designer, the head of the makeup department, and a wardrobe man and lady.

I must have gotten the part. The same inane dialogue went on at RKO as it did at Warner's. And the next thing I know, I'm shooting a movie called *Love for Bail*. A nice little story. Every studio in those days had one or two of those scripts deep in their grouch bags. The cost was right, between four and five hundred thousand per picture, and they always managed to get at least two names to help sell it. These pictures were called "programmers." The biggest difference between a "programmer" and an "epic" was the expense of shlepping the cannon over the mountain. This one was the story of three kids who grew up in Hell's Kitchen. That's the kind of neighborhood where you grow up to be either a gangster, a cop, or a priest. The leads in the picture were George Raft, Pat O'Brien, and Jim Backus. So guess who played what. The fact that they were at least twenty years older than I was didn't seem to bother anyone in the least. Besides, we were made up like Kabuki dancers.

Three or four days before a picture rolls, it is customary for an actor to drop in on the producer to discuss the character he is about to play. As if by chance, it just so happens the director also drops in and, as if by chance, the makeup people and the wardrobe man and woman, the script clerk, and some other members of the cast also drop in—as if by chance. If the producer had actually called any of us and had asked us to appear in his office at a specific time, then he would be obliged to give us a pro rata payment. It occurred to me that it would be possible to eke out a living just by knowing all the ramifications of the Screen Actors Guild contract and really abiding by them!

As if by chance, a buffet table had been set up in the office. It is a well-known fact that actors will go anywhere, do anything, for a ham on rye and a prune Danish. There were also, as if by chance, and courtesy of Howard Hughes, three large-breasted ladies available to those with assigned parking and at least "fifteen-hundred dollars on a three-week guarantee."

I tried my best to act as if this were old hat, and to hide the fact that this was only my second picture, when in reality it was white knuckle and bug-eyed time! We were just getting to know each other when the door opened and the ebullient Pat O'Brien danced in, lustily singing "The Tam O'Shanter Ball," followed by an ominous George Raft with his patent leather shoes and his patent leather hair, whereupon at least a dozen photographers appeared from out of nowhere—as if by chance.

"Stand over by Mr. Raft. That's good, Mr. O'Brien. You, too, Mr. Backus."

While the snapping went on, Pat gave out with a gaggle of Irish stories. It was typical of Pat, whom I knew rather well. George Raft turned to shake my hand and gave me his famous laser-beam stare. I have been looked in the eye by experts, but this one could stop a Sherman tank in its tracks. George Raft wasn't discovered on a drugstore stool. He hadn't been a hit in the theatre. He wasn't even an actor. They just found him one day on the doorstep of RKO. . . . Like the baby Moses he, too, came out of the rushes. Who made him a star? Was it a giant joke or a political ploy staged by Joe Kennedy? Could it have been that oil guy with the sneakers? He simply emerged a full-fledged star with the correct wardrobe, the correct house, the right car, even the requisite combination stand-in/bodyguard—all the accouterments of a movie star at their most blatant. But when they gave him his first movie (the part was a little gem—the kind we actors would die for), he came through. The picture was *Scar Face*, starring the great Paul Muni, no less. Yet to this day, ask anyone who was the star of *Scar Face*—ask them the name of the guy who, when he got shot, slowly sank down with those agate eyes blazing while he continued flipping that coin till he hit the floor and died—ask anyone. Sure, maybe some rum-soaked trivia expert might blurt out, "Paul Muni." Just tell him to keep right on drinking his C. and C. with the water back, then ignore him. We know that any way you look at it, Raft was *really* the star—a new star to be reckoned with.

Working with George Raft on *Love for Bail* was a pleasure. He was a gentleman, he showed up on time, and he knew all his lines. He knew his part, your part, my part—he memorized the whole script. I once asked him why he was never late like many other stars, and why he bothered to learn the whole script, and he replied, "I have to, I don't have any talent."

We had finally finished the first week of shooting—all tough locations. I had just gotten home. I was greeted by Henny with a lusty kiss, and we were just starting our sit-com dialogue when the phone rang. It was my agent Al.

"Pussycat? Guess what?"

"Don't tell me we're shutting down," I kidded.

"That's right! The big guy doesn't like the ingenue. No boobs. So they're going to recast. Don't worry. Go play some golf. You're on salary."

I began to think this was the norm. What a great business! Was this the way it was always done?

In the meantime, I made pictures. Suddenly I was in great demand. I went from one movie to another. Don't let anyone tell you it's not hard work. Up at five. Home at six-thirty or seven, often totally wiped out. I loved it! But there was one thing wrong. I got typed. Instead of playing comedy roles as I had in radio, for some unknown reason I was always cast as the hero's best friend. I guess the whole thing started when I was best friend to Fred MacMurray in *Father Was a Fullback*. Then came Joe Cotton's best friend in *The Man with a Cloak*. And Jeff Chandler's in *The Iron Man*, and Donald O'Connor's in *I Love Melvin*, then Kirk Douglas's in *Top Secret Affair*. I even played a Roman best friend to Victor Mature in *Androcles and the Lion*. And these are just a few!

It took years to overcome the "best friend" stigma. I guess it was *Rebel Without a Cause* that broke the cycle. At least I didn't have to go on those jaunts with Al to see the "boys" in person in order to nail down a part. They knew who I was by now. There was even a type of role known in the trade as "a Jim Backus part." As a matter of fact, this almost cost me my chance to play the lead in one of the first television comedy series. When Joan Davis was casting for a leading man for *I Married Joan*, my name came up. "Oh, no," she said. "Not Jim Backus.

He could never play comedy. Everyone knows he's a straight actor!''

They say lightning never strikes twice. In my case it not only struck twice, it struck three times! Al no longer had to take me by the hand and play those stupid games with me. I was a big boy now. Occasionally I had to test for a part, but that's all. If I got it, fine. If I didn't, maybe another one would come along.

I had just tested for a role at Twentieth Century-Fox that week when I got a phone call from the studio telling me to be in Darryl Zanuck's office at three that afternoon. Alone! No agents! Darryl Zanuck's office? Alone?

The great man was seated behind a desk you could land a helicopter on. He was dressed in a paramilitary style, a sort of combination General Patton and John Wayne, and swinging a polo mallet, making broad swipes in the general direction of my bread basket. He talked. I didn't. He went on to say that he liked my test, that I got the part, that he had always liked my work ever since my first part in *Father Was a Fullback*, that there were roles coming up in future pictures that only I could play, and that he was going to talk to Al about a long-term contract. He then threw me a salute with his mallet and swung his chair around in a full circle, which meant that the interview was over and if I had a rebuttal to do it somewhere else. I must say I left that office walking on air. It may seem silly, but all I could think about was that Tyrone Power was on that same lot and now maybe I'd get my ninety cents back!

The picture was *Half Angel*, starring Loretta Young and Joe Cotton. We had been shooting for a week now, mostly in downtown Los Angeles—a place as foreign to a Beverly Hills resident as the other side of the moon. I was lying in my trailer in that delicious euphoric state, not quite asleep and semi-aware of my surroundings. I remember how hot it was, and I remember lying there for what seemed like hours waiting to be called for the next shot. As I started to awaken, I was aware that I was lying on what passed for a couch in the back of my little portable dressing room. I could feel that inevitable piece of Kleenex tucked into my collar by the wardrobe man to keep my makeup from soiling my shirt.

There were stirrings—movements in the room. I opened one eye. It was my stand-in, Bob Harris. Faithful Bob—a pain in the ass, not too bright, but dependable. Before I ever came to Hollywood I thought that a stand-in was a double, a look-alike. Wrong! A stand-in does just that. He stands in for you so they can do all that adjusting of the lights, which gives the "first team" time to study lines, rehearse, have costume fittings, or whatever. Bob had been around the business forever in every capacity. He was a former chorus boy, now technically an extra. He had been assigned to me on my very first picture. Bob just happened to be there. Bob always just happened to be everywhere. I had to admit grudgingly to myself that all I had learned about camera angles, key lights, how to protect myself in a scene, all that movie technique sneered at by New York actors—I had learned from Bob.

"You can go back to sleep now, boss. They won't get to you for another half hour. I checked with the gaffer."

"Then why the hell did they get me here at the crack of dawn? I only have that one scene left."

"The light was wrong," said Bob. "They'll get to you right after lunch. You'll be through by three o'clock. The coffee man told me."

Bob got his information from the goddamnedest sources. I dozed off again. I was inured to the noise of the 1950 movie-making going on right outside my trailer—laying down dolly tracks, the crews shouting, "Move that reflector!" "Kill that brute!" What the hell, I remember thinking, I might as well get up and take another look at the script.

My feet hit the deck and the trailer swayed. The ever-alert, cheerful Bob charged in. The trailer bowed and grunted in protest. In his arms was a freshly pressed shirt. He was always doing chores—whether necessary or not. He made it look busy.*

"Boss, have I got good news for you!"

I knew Bob and his good news. I yawned. "What's the good news?"

"Well, boss, between you and I, you know a lot of people didn't want Julie Dassen directing this picture in the first place. They feel, and I agree with them, that he's a no good pinko . . . a Commie . . . a . . ."

"Hold it!" I shouted. "Hold it right there! I know you and I don't see eye to eye politically. If you feel that Mr. Dassen is a Communist, say so! Don't use those Parnell Thomas cuties, 'pinko,' 'Commie'! I happen to think that Julie Dassen is one hell of a director. Besides, what do his political leanings, if any, have to do with this piece of shit we're making?"

The unchastened Bob got very busy. He emptied ashtrays and hung things up. "Well, in view of what happened today, a lot of people, when they heard the news, refused to work with him anymore and walked off the picture—"

"Wait a minute! Back up! Not so fast! *What* happened today?"

"Well, boss, you've been in here sleeping. You haven't heard. We're at war with North Korea!" I guess he saw my stricken face. "But don't worry, President Truman says it's not a real war. It's only a police action. So, boss, you go get your car. I'll have all your clothes and things ready to put in the trunk. They fired Dassen, the picture's wrapping, we're shut down till they get another director."

It had really happened. We were shut down. Julie Dassen just disappeared. Later we heard that he was in Greece,

---

*"Make it look busy": A command given to the extras just before the camera turns reminding them to "Eat Up—Smoke it up!—Chat up a storm!" In other words, "Look alive!"

married to Melina Mercouri. He became internationally known through his direction of *Never on Sunday* and *Topkapi*, among others. I never saw him again.

As I exited the trailer, the voice of the second assistant called from the door of the set. "Mr. Backus, you're wanted on the phone."

I grabbed it and put it to my ear. "Hey, bubbie!" It was Al. "Great news!"

"I know, Al. I'm here where it happened!"

"It'll be at least four weeks," said Al. "Play golf, relax. Take Henny to Magnin's. . . . But do me one favor. Don't get a tan!"

I Married Joan

Trying to be a friend of Joan Davis's was like watching your mother-in-law go over a cliff in your brand-new Rolls.

I costarred with Joan in the situation comedy *I Married Joan* for the better part of four years. Although we shot these shows in the early fifties, they now have cult status, thanks to the current reruns on cable.

Compared to any other form of entertainment, this is by far the most exhausting, physically and emotionally. I'd just like to give you a few pertinent facts that the average viewer never realizes. This is entirely from an actor's viewpoint. What the writers, directors, and producers go through is another story.

First of all, there is the great mental strain, because no matter how you slice it, you have to learn the words. In our kind of show, there was no reading from Tele-PrompTers or even "idiot cards." I'm sure that by now even the most naïve viewer realizes that those shy, downward glances by his favorite entertainer are sneaky readings of the script off giant cards. On the other hand, there is another style of reading, which was practiced by Jack Webb and his celebrated *Dragnet* company. When you saw those big head close-ups, the characters were reading from

TelePrompTers. These were rolls of script in huge type that were slowly unreeled for the actor. They were well illuminated and placed above the camera. On our show, which was a fast-moving comedy, neither of these methods was practical, so we had to do it the hard way. We had to learn it—every word! Every week!

Our average script ran fifty-five pages. This means that in three years I memorized approximately 6,545 pages of dialogue, which is equivalent to memorizing *War and Peace* and *Gone With the Wind*. I remember the first couple of months Joan and I used to stare at each other and say, "This is impossible. We just can't do it." It never got easy, but it's a lot like going on the wagon—the first few months are the hardest. How I used to envy Joan, who had one of those photographic memories. Finally, after a while, she was able to look at the script and she had it! With me it was touch-and-go the whole way.

Learning the words was actually only about one-third of it. Ours was what is known in the trade as a "physical" show. We never had a quiet scene where we sat in the living room while I read the paper and she calmly knitted. Many times we started out that way, but on our show she naturally had to get tangled up in the yarn or else she knitted me to the sofa. If one of us went to the closet for a piece of clothing, the door jammed and we had to climb out through the transom. Or we went on a trip and had to spend the night in a Murphy bed—but in our case, Murphy was still in it!

Our show always ended on a wild, spectacular comedy note. There was the time we made popcorn in the kitchen and, thanks to the script, the popcorn machine went wild and we wound up literally wallowing around in six feet of popcorn. Or the time Joan visited a famous chef and found herself in a giant kettle of stew. Or the one with the turn-about masquerade. I went dressed as a woman and Joan went as Satan, and her tail caught fire! These prop stunts were very hard to do, and there was always an element of physical danger. There was a registered nurse on the set at all times, and she saw plenty of service. Due to this type of work, our insurance rate was up there with steeplejacks, test pilots, and deep-sea divers. Neither of us ever used doubles and Joan did some of the most amazing stunts I have ever seen. Once she worked on wires thirty-five feet above the set—without a net! I was once thrown from an electric horse . . . my head went through a wall.

On our show the billing—which is the lifeblood of every actor—should have said, "Starring Joan Davis and Jim Backus." But when the credits came on, they read, "Starring Joan Davis *with* Jim Backus." That little word "with" made all the difference. It meant that Joan was the star and I was an indentured servant. What it really meant was that she owned the show and she called the shots. I was the only guy in town who came home with lipstick on his paycheck! But—as my Aunt Cora would have said—it was steady.

Joan wasn't the only boss-lady at the studio. General Service Studio, where we shot the series, was a matriarchy. There was Lucille Ball, Ann Sothern, Eve Arden, Gracie Allen, and Harriet Nelson, to name a few. Instead of a wall around the studio, they should have had a giant girdle.

In those early days of television we were sailing in uncharted waters. There were no precedents to fall back on, no traditions or folk heroes to revere. The stage had its Garricks and Booths, the cinema its Fairbankses and Chaplins; all *we* had were *Captain Kangaroo*s and *Howdy Doody*s. The guidelines for our show had already been set by those martini-swilling founding fathers on Madison Avenue, who were in turn protecting the tender interests of Ford, U. S. Steel, and I.J. Farben. We were saddled with a list of no-no's a mile long—the Puritan ethic updated. All that was lacking was stocks, a ducking stool, and a scarlet letter for those who had impure thoughts about Arthur Godfrey.

I Married Joan was set somewhere in lobotomy land. I

played the part of Judge Bradley J. Stevens who, in a moment of blinding insanity, had married a thoroughly disarranged airline stewardess played, of course, by Joan Davis.

She spent the next four years making a complete horse's ass of Brad, perpetrating such horrendous tricks on her poor, befogged spouse as to make her eligible for a stint on Devil's Island—or even Gilligan's! Brad, who hadn't the jurisprudence to judge a dog show, loved every moment of it, as he went about ladling out his own brand of treacly justice—"Whereas, who gets custody of the pony?"

The scripts for *I Married Joan* were conceived by the "boys." At that time, the writers of all the comedy shows were called "boys," regardless of literary achievement, age, or education—a hangover from radio. Among our "boys" were Neil Simon, Abe Burrows, Sherwood Schwartz, and Leon Uris. The writers' office was, of course, known as "the boys' room."

Joan had literally never read anything but comedy scripts, so *all* writers of *any* sort were "boys" to her. When I told her that I was spending my summer hiatus by going back to the theatre to play *The Man Who Came to Dinner*, she said, "Oh, yes, that was written by those two Broadway boys." When I informed her that one of its authors was a boy named George S. Kaufman, who had gotten a Pulitzer Prize, she replied, "That's shit compared to an Emmy!" But, despite her ignorance of the world outside of show business and her lack of education, her knowledge of comedy construction was nothing short of miraculous. Her judgment of what would play was infallible. Her ability to come up with a surprise ending, a tag, or a snapper was on a par with Jack Benny's. Comedy writing simply cannot be taught. If it could, gag writing might become a cottage industry. Joan's unerring comedic instincts came from those endless one-night stands in vaudeville, going from one tank town to another, polishing and polishing a joke or a piece of business until it shone like a Kimberley diamond.

Joan was a strict taskmaster of the unwritten commandments of comedy. She knew all the comedic yardsticks, some as old as the Pyramids—or Henny Youngman's jokes. One of the commandments was the law of three. For example, "Winkin', Blinkin', and Nod," or "healthy, wealthy, and wise," or "The Atcheson, Topeka, and the Santa Fe." If you stop after "Topeka," the rhythm is off. If you add the New York Central, you've gone too far.

She knew that certain words would get a laugh and others would not. I soon learned that "pickles" was funny; "relish" was not. "Seven" was funny; "eight" was not. "Cleveland" was funny; "Pittsburgh" was not. And, to break the rule of three, here is a fourth commandment: "Saks" for some reason is funny; "Magnin's" is not.

Every show had a standard opening. It opened on the Judge (me) arriving home after a hard day in his chambers. He opened the door and made an entrance. They *never* showed him arriving in his car. If the car was visible, that would knock out rerun sales to all other makes of cars. . . . And so on, all the way down the line. We lived in a brandless vacuum, except for the complete G. E. kitchen. General Electric just happened to be our sponsor.

After I entered the house on *I Married Joan*, my business was invariably as follows: The lovable Judge would take off his homburg, place it on the hall table along with his briefcase, and then trumpet in the general direction of the model G. E. kitchen, "Oh, Joan, I'm home! What's for dinner?" It was head on! Never any Darien foreplay like "Let's have a drink," or, "How about a quick hump before dinner?" So Joan would invariably reply, "Your favorite dishes, dear. Pot roast with potato pancakes and sour cream." For a nonsectarian WASP, the Judge subsisted entirely on the ethnic fare of a Hassidic rabbi. In the move from Bensonhurst to the Hills of Beverly, the "boys" had not altered their dietary habits. Once, the Judge brought home a political figure he was currying favor with, and the "boys" had written Joan a welcoming line, "Have a piece fruit, State Senator. . . . A tangerine wouldn't kill you."

Sensing a problem, the sponsors sent a man of impeccable breeding and uncertain gender posthaste to act as technical adviser to the "boys" on the Stevens' life-style. He withdrew the Judge from latkes, tmsiss, and flanken to the world of soufflés, mousse, and quiche. (Note the rule of three.)

I spent four years working with Joan—twelve to fourteen hours a day—five days a week—forty-one weeks a year. More time than I spent at home. At such close proximity, you get to know each other pretty well, and, like a marriage, you have to adjust. Professionally, she was a joy. Off camera, it was a different story. I find it difficult to write about her with any continuity. Because she had no continuity.

Joan knew every joke ever written. Since I am pretty good at them myself, we were able to communicate by simply using tag lines of jokes. She had a biting sense of humor. For example, on one show we had a guest star who was a would-be Clark Gable. Joan eyed him appraisingly as he flexed his muscles and flashed his teeth around the set. He had to perform what he considered a hazardous stunt. He was to enter through a window all of six feet off the ground. He looked it over and said, "Miss Davis, I'm going to need a cup!" (an athletic supporter). She appraised him carefully and replied, "From what I can see, all you'll need is a demitasse."

Fat Phil was one of the writers on the *I Married Joan* show. He was unnecessarily obese, thanks to his wife's jealousy. She plied him with calories, thinking this would make him unattractive to Joan or any lady who might be in the market for a short, fat, ugly gag writer. Since he lived five short blocks from the studio, he had very little driving to do. When he arrived in his driveway, his green-eyed spouse would dash out and feel his radiator, and it had better be cool! If it was warm, she was convinced that he had traveled more than his allotted distance for a romantic dalliance, and then all hell would break loose!

One Monday, at the regular weekly reading of the script, Phil suddenly announced that he was on a diet and this time he meant it! He raved on about how wonderful he felt and how he was bound and determined to lose twenty pounds in two weeks' time. "Think I'm kidding?" Nobody answered him. We had heard it all before. "Okay, okay," he shouted. "A thousand bucks says I do it!" It was one of those hypothetical bets like, "My old man can lick your old man!"—but not to Joan! She looked at him through her calculating lynx eyes. "A thousand says you don't!"

Two weeks to the day—same time, same place, and another reading—Joan was in her usual seat, at the head of a long conference table flanked by the "boys." Standing behind her was the studio nurse with an ominous hospital scale. Staring at this in terror was Fat Phil, fatter than ever. "Okay," said Joan, "before we read, get your ass up on the scale." There was a hush as a protesting Phil mounted the scale. To Fat Phil's chagrin, and to no one's surprise, he was three pounds heavier. "Gee, Joan, I was only kidding!" he whined. "I wasn't," hissed our star. That month his paycheck was one thousand dollars lighter.

Joan's behavior was enough to make a psychiatrist hit the couch. Her psyche, if indeed she had one, was as uncharted as the Sargasso Sea. Some of her actions were obvious to any drawing room analyst. For example, Lucille Ball was to Joan Davis what Moriarity was to Sherlock Holmes. One day she read in the *Hollywood Reporter* that Lucy was going to do a film called *The Long Long Trailer*, all about high jinks in a mobile home. This was accompanied by a photograph of Miss Ball in front of an endless, fully appointed mobile home. The next day a longer trailer than Lucy's arrived on the lot to serve as Joan's portable dressing room. To get this ten-wheeled behemoth on the sound stage necessitated knocking out a wall and using part of another stage. Then the wall had to be rebuilt around the trailer, as the lack of it caused a sound leak. Besides three huge rooms, this mobile monster had a wet bar and a septic tank bidet—a first in mobile hygiene!

Long after the show was canceled, long after we had left, long after Joan had completely forgotten all about her huge toy, it just sat there. It wasn't until a conglomerate bought the studio that they had money enough to move it out and at long last properly fix the wall.

During the making of *I Love Lucy*, Lucy became pregnant. The headlines blared: "LUCY TO HAVE A BABY!" To make it even more newsworthy, it was announced that they would portray Lucy's entire pregnancy up to the actual birth right on the show. Talk about a first! The Neilson ratings ballooned along with Lucy's tummy. For nine months Joan was in a seething rage. "How could they do this to me?" she whined. The "boys" cowered in their hutches. Then I noticed a strange look in her eyes, a ray of lust! My God, it was pointed in my direction! Was the rumor true? Had my burritos been laced with ginseng root? Was she about to evoke the *droit-de-signora*? I ran to the producer. "Sorry, Jim, my hands are tied," he told me. I ran to the director. He fell about with laughter. I ran to my dear, true, only friends—the "boys." And one of them came up with an idea. He sold her on doing a show about artificial insemination. "Think of the comedic possibilities, Joan! Switching test tubes . . . misplaced sperm . . . Mahatma Gandhi, the accidental father!" She loved it. There would be diaper jokes by the mile!

On the *I Married Joan* show we had a feathered, furry, or scaly guest star just about every other week. In one episode we were supposed to be spending a weekend in a friend's mountain cabin. Joan, in her usual scatterbrained way, was supposed to have forgotten to pack the supplies. We were to arrive to find the cabin empty and the cupboards bare, and at that point my car battery was supposed to go dead. So there we were—stranded. I'll spare you the entire plot —Chaplin did it better. But in the next scene we were starving—out of our minds with hunger—and were to be discovered carving a hot water bottle which we were to eat daintily with great relish. Suddenly, according to the script, we were both supposed to see a huge turtle. As one, we were to pounce on it, and the turtle was to evade us and lead us on a not-so-merry chase. In the next scene we were to be eating turtle soup. Okay? Well, that's the way the "boys" wrote it. It's not the way we played it! We just couldn't get that turtle to evade us. He wouldn't move. He just sat there, or whatever it is turtles do. At this point, I must tell you that when Joan worked, she *worked*! And she expected everyone else on the set to do the same. Also, she treated animals like fellow performers. (She once had a two-week feud with a canary.) So when the turtle ignored us and refused to cooperate, she screamed at it. It continued to just sit there and stare. She tried bribing it. It still wouldn't move. The turtle simply would not budge. "Okay," she yelled, "you son of a bitch! You'll never work for me again!"

Once, on another episode, we had a scene with a chimp. It was a dream sequence. It had something to do with a sultan (me) and a harem girl (Joan) all done up in bits of gauze and gold chains, and a chimp who was dressed as a medieval court jester. The two-toned doublet over his rubber pants and the bells on his foolscap drove him crazy! Furthermore, he kept dropping his wand. Joan hated him! Not only because he was holding up production, but also because she had once been bitten on the canetta by a chimp in a long-ago movie and had never gotten over it. She was terrified of its happening again. "Those little bastards can kill you!" she complained. "Don't ever turn your back on the little shit. He'll bite you right on the keister. Their bite is pure poison. Like a rattler!" she cautioned. "Keep away from that little putz!" All I had to do was sit on my sultan's throne, while Joan had all sorts of complicated business with the chimp. The poor little overcostumed animal was getting more and more exhausted and confused. Joan, with her low threshold of tolerance, kept getting crankier and crankier. Finally it worked! The miracle happened! A take! Then the glorious cry from the director: "Cut! Print! That's it! It's a take! It's a wrap!"

Wearily I climbed down from my throne after a long, horrible, tedious day of the chimp and his wand and Joan and her complaints about being bitten and poisoned by the fuzzy little guest star. As we were saying a very weary good night, the chimp slowly and slyly walked over to Joan, squeezed in between us, and reached up and bit her on the navel. She was *right*! He *did* bite her! They rushed her to the hospital screaming all the way. "What did I tell you? Those little cockers are poison! I'll die! I'll die! I just know it!"

Well, they did everything they could for her. Put her to bed, sterilized the wound, gave her a tetanus shot, kept her overnight—the works! Joan recovered, but believe it or not, three days later the chimp died.

For the star of a show consistently in the top ten, Joan kept a very low profile. The public knew very little about her, nothing at all about her private life. Joan didn't care. Her fear of interviews was phobic. So to the public she was just that madcap girl they saw on their little home screen. As a matter of fact, for many years she was able to have a sustained affair with one of America's most beloved comedians. And not only did the public never find out about it, neither did his wife and five daughters!

One day we were informed that our sponsors from Schenectady wanted to have a corporate hoedown in Los Angeles for the top brass. Their wives desired only one thing—to have cocktails in Joan's Bel Air home. Joan put her little Delman-shod foot down. "No way!" she growled. The then top echelon NBC con men were immediately summoned. They pointed out that G.E. was paying her some $40,000 a week and it could only go up. They assured her that these electronic nabobs and their spouses would stay no longer than one hour—and as an added incentive they promised her that G. E. would air-condition her whole house and redo her kitchen with all the latest appliances. They would even throw in an egg timer for me!

A much softened Joan agreed. "But only an hour!" she snarled. This was just dandy with the NBC executives, as they well knew—as we all did—that Joan had a three-drink tolerance. One drop over that and she lashed out at the nearest target like a crazed asp.

Everything was smooth as silk at the cocktail hour. The sponsors, complete with their better halves, arrived in a covey of limos. Joan, looking almost angelic in a pink organdy Dior, was at her most ingratiating.

At the end of the hour the executive in charge of the tour glanced in horror at Joan nuzzling her drink. "Come on, folks!" He hustled them into a group. "We don't want to be late for dinner at the Coconut Grove, do we?" He was aware that Joan had put a head, a "little shooter" as she called it, on her third drink. She shook hands graciously with the sponsor and his wife. There the lady stood—a tower of chiffon, a festival of ruffles, a gala of geegaws and buttons and bows. Joan looked her over with those little agate eyes, and through her Medici smile she purred, "Ohhh! I see your mother's been sewing again!"

She never got the kitchen.

My egg timer works just fine, thank you.

This Is Henny . . .

Joan was not exactly my best friend. We really had nothing in common, especially in the sense-of-humor department. For one thing, she loved to have people think that she was really married to Jim—probably because it drove me crazy, as it always made me out to be the other woman. I played her girlfriend Harriet on the show, and professionally I found her to be warm, talented, and giving. In other words, a total professional. Socially, although we were constantly thrown together, we had very little to say to each other.

Once Joan and Jim were making a personal appearance in Louisville. I was not invited to attend. I understood that. It was all part of the game. (Advice: If you're thinking of marrying an actor, you'd better do a little stint in show business yourself or you'll never understand his pressures and obligations, or indeed any part of his job, and you won't survive, baby!) They arrived late and, as Joan and Jim were checking into the hotel, the confused room clerk looked up from the hotel registry he had been consulting and said, "There must be some mistake, Your Honor. You're in Room 219 and your wife here is in 517, 518, 519, 520, 521, and 522. I've heard of separate rooms, but separate floors?" Joan took her fistful of keys and winked at him and said, "He snores!"

I heard the story from Jim, who thought it was hilarious. I didn't. So I decided to pay him back. Jim and I were doing a sudden personal appearance in Scranton. I was the last-minute substitute for Joan. The entire stunt happened so suddenly that we were not even preregistered in the hotel. As we approached the desk, I managed to get in back of Jim and walk a few respectful paces behind him, at the same time surreptitiously removing my wedding ring. I stood quietly in back of him while he rang the little bell to attract the desk clerk. The clerk looked up from his racing form and a large smile spread across his face as he came forth. "Well, well, it's the Judge! What'll it be, Judge?" he continued, never once taking his disapproving eyes off me. "Do you want a big bed or twins?"

"Wait a minute," Jim replied. "I'll ask her. Darling—" He turned, located me, and continued. "What'll it be? A big bed or twins?"

With my eyes modestly downcast, I murmured, "Oh, it doesn't matter to me, sir!" (Advice: Although marriage may be a gift from God, you have to do your own maintenance.)

The last words I ever said to Joan were unprintable. And why not? I am not a fan of small scurrying animals, and that week the script called for a mouse. We all appealed to her.

"Not a shot of the mouse, Joan! People will turn off their sets!"

"You don't really have to show it, Joan!"

"Actually, Joan, all you have to do is indicate it!"

But she was adamant. Why? Who knows! Maybe Lucy had a mouse on her show that week. Since I was only in the first and mouseless scene, I was dismissed early. I was lucky. It was hot that day and the lights didn't help. I could hardly wait to get out of there before the mouse did its scene and to get home for a swim. As I was picking up my bag from my dressing table, I noticed in my nearsighted way that there seemed to be two large mason jars in front of my mirror. I leaned over to take a closer look. I couldn't believe my eyes, so I leaned in farther. Suddenly I realized, after a lot of squinting, that there were two hideous gray mice on my dressing table—each in its own jar! I spun around in disgust and saw, lurking in my doorway, Joan—smiling her special butter-wouldn't-melt-in-hermouth smile. "I knew you were leaving early," she cooed. "And the poor mouse doesn't have a dressing room."

I was so taken aback that I blurted, "Why are there two of them?"

She pulled herself up to her full height and, with her nasal Minnesota twang in full orbit, she answered as she pointed. "One is his stand-in."

This Is Jim . . .

I Married Joan was a huge hit and Joan made a lot of money. She also *had* a lot of money! At one time Joan

Davis was the highest-paid lady entertainer in the world. Henny will bear me out when I tell you that, among other things, she had a walk-in closet full of fur coats, and she had jewelry by the vaultful. What can you give to someone who has everything? What could I give her for Christmas? Joan had an offbeat sense of humor, so I decided on a photograph in an always-appreciated sterling silver frame. I engaged the still gallery, where they make the portraits and publicity shots of the stars ... like Walter Cronkite as Santa Claus with a huge sack of toys, or Ed Sullivan as Father Time, or Alistair Cooke with fur ears emerging from an egg to celebrate the Lenten season.

So we decided that what would amuse Joan most was me doing a cheesecake nude. The first Christmas I wore mesh stockings, a waist cinch, and a Marlene Dietrich wig. The next year I grew bolder and wore western boots, a cowboy hat, and a holster covering my gun. The third Christmas I turned my nude back to the camera and provocatively dropped a silver fox over my lower cleavage. These were beautifully done in the most professional manner. Joan loved them! She put them on her piano right next to Ike, Bishop Sheen, and Sister Kenny.

Joan lived across the road from us. Her house burned to the ground on the last day of the celebrated Bel Air fire in 1963. When the firemen arrived, they found no one home and did their usual ax job. They proceeded to drag out the furniture, including the piano with the three nude pictures of me still on the top. At that very moment I ran up the road from our house to see if I could be of any assistance. Well, the firemen looked at me, then at the pictures, then at me. ... Need I say more?

Fire seems to have played a macabre role in Joan Davis's star-crossed life. During the filming of the series she barely escaped with her life when her bed caught fire. When I asked her if she was alone at the time, she replied with typical Davis candor, "No, there was Pierre, a French aviator who went down in flames."

A few years after her Bel Air house was completely ravaged by fire, her mother, her daughter, and her only two grandchildren perished in a fire that engulfed her Palm Springs house.

It was boiling hot. I hadn't slept a wink. The dress rehearsal had been endless and difficult, and the hotel air-conditioning had broken down. Who ever expected a heat wave like this? The natives took it right in their stride. Why should 1961 be different from any other Milwaukee summer?

I was opening that night at the ballroom downstairs and I was exhausted. I finally managed to cork off, only to be awakened by the loudest, shrillest telephone bell I'd ever heard. I sat up in bed, wondering for a moment where I was. . . . And where was the damn phone, anyway? I found it on Henny's side and staggered over to catch it before it screamed again.

A voice said, "Mr. Backus?"

"Who is this," I shouted, "waking me in the middle of the night?!"

I looked at the clock. It was 7:05.

"Sorry, Mr. Backus, but it's after nine here in New York. This is James Bacon with AP. I just wanted to know if you have any comment on the death of Joan Davis?"

And that's how I found out that she had passed away.

After *I Married Joan* was canceled in 1955, Joan spent all of her time in her Palm Springs house, and we never saw or heard from her again. She became a recluse, and there were mumblings that she was quite ill—a heart ailment. There was no way of reaching her. She communicated with no one.

But I was in for a surprise. The summer before I played Milwaukee, I opened at the Slate Brothers to break in my act for Las Vegas. This charming little boîte was the gathering place for all the glitzy Hollywood types—rounders, agents, call girls, predatory comedians, and stars on the prowl, among others—in short, the "in" group. If an act scored here, then Vegas was a piece of cake. This was my first time out as a stand-up comedian, and each show I did (three a night) was a trial by fire.

One night, as I was standing in what passed for "the wings," one of the more articulate Slate Brothers hissed in my ear, "Hey, schmuck, you better be good."

"Why?" I asked.

"Your partner's out there."

I swiveled around in a cold sweat. "Who?" I asked, although I already knew.

"Who else," he told me, "Joan Davis! I gave her a good table."

I sneaked a quick look out front, and there she was at a ringside table. Her escort was a stout lady in a crisp white uniform . . . no men. Just Joan and her Florence Nightingale. Then it hit me, what if she had already gone past her third drink? I could hear her shouting, "Tell the Feen-a-Mint story!" Oh, God, what if she jumped up on the stage! Stage? It was more like a wooden auction block. They must have once auctioned off slaves here. Too late! A drum roll and I was on.

Since this upholstered sewer, which had formerly been a pet shop, could seat no more than sixty people, I was only about ten feet from the farthest customer. On Saturday nights they had bar stools in the alley and people watched the show through the windows. It was intimate and al fresco at the same time. I switched my act to automatic pilot and took another look at Joan. She looked much thinner. She smiled up at me rather wistfully, not her usual curled-lip number, but a rather sweet, sad smile. I started my routine. She laughed in all the right places, not attention-getting yaks, but with genuine sincerity. Not that cued, "I can't stand it anymore" braying that was *de rigueur* when Don Rickles or Sammy Davis, Jr., are performing. At one point I referred to *The Joan Davis Show*. This caused the audience to crane their necks to see her reactions. She rose ever so slightly, gave the joke a slight chuckle—which is all it deserved—and gave the audience a nod worthy of Sir Herbert Beerbohm Tree. The rest of the act was as smooth as cream, thanks to Joan.

After the show I raced out front as fast as I could get there. I caught her just outside the door about to get into a limousine. Her sturdy uniformed companion was guiding her ever so subtly. "Joannie," I called, "wait a minute." She was already in the car. "Thanks for coming. You didn't have to, you know."

"What do you mean, I didn't have to?" She smiled from her seat in the limo. "I had to check out my costar, didn't I?" (Now she tells me!) "You were wonderful, but I wish you'd tell the Feen-a-Mint joke."

"Promise me you'll come to Las Vegas," I said.

"I will if I can get away from Captain Bligh." She indicated her plump companion with the comfortable shoes who was just getting in on the other side. Joan held out her hand. I kissed it.

"Good-bye, Joan. Thank you for coming."

"Good-bye, Brad." She used my *Joan Davis Show* name. And as the limousine started to roll, she leaned out of the window and said, "Tell Henny I'm sorry."

The *Rebel*

I first met James Dean on Thanksgiving night of 1954, before *East of Eden* had been released, and, frankly, at that time I'd never heard of him. Since Henny was out of town, Sharley and Keenan Wynn, knowing I would be alone, asked me to come to their house and share a turkey. They explained that they were inviting a few other lonely bachelors. Said bachelors included Rod Steiger, Ralph Meeker, Arthur Loew, Jr., and a rather small young man who didn't look a day over eighteen. He was dressed in a navy blue suit that looked as if he had worn it to his confirmation, plus a black shirt, black boots with buckles, and a pair of oversized horned-rimmed glasses held together with adhesive tape.

I felt sorry for this strange kid because he seemed ill at ease. As it always is with actors, the conversation was mainly about show business, which he never entered into. The only time he spoke up was when, as it often did at the Wynns', the talk turned to racing cars and motorcycles. After the other guests had departed, I lingered on and remember saying to Keenan, "It was sweet of you and Sharley to have all of us lost souls over for dinner, but don't you think that that kid who works in a garage was uncomfortable with all of us hams?"

"Works in a garage? Are you kidding?" said Keenan. "I saw a preview of that new picture *East of Eden*, and that kid you called a garage mechanic is so brilliant in it he tore the theatre apart." Four months later, I was signed to play the "garage mechanic's" father.

This was shortly after my stint in *I Married Joan*. Three long years of "Joannie, I'm home. What's for dinner?" Three years of "Joannie, you mailed a letter with what! My Mozambique Purple? What'll I tell the boys down at my stamp club?" Three years of total emasculation—Desi Arnaz without the drum. I was now at a new low on the self-esteem meter. There I was, at the gates of General Service Studios in a new suit, with a five-dollar bill and a letter from the warden.

Al, my faithful agent, was waiting. He took me to a restaurant. It was nice to have lunch where the soup wasn't wired and the waitress wasn't a four-hundred-pound gorilla. As you can see, I was walking a fine line between fact and fiction.

While we were walking to Al's car, after a nice placid lunch, I noticed something strange. People were staring at me. I checked my zipper. A lady reprimanded her kid for pointing at me. I felt naked and vulnerable. Then it dawned on me with the clarity of a raindrop. I was a star! It had happened! Suddenly it made sense. Radio? Complete anonymity. Movies? The eternal faceless best friend. Someone shoved a piece of paper at me. I signed it. "Jim Backus." No, no! That's not my name! I crossed it out and wrote "Judge Bradley J. Stevens." This was to be the albatross around my neck. My pact with the devil. I had sold out. Never would I have the chance to say, "Frankly, my dear, I don't give a damn!" "I coulda been a contendah!" "Of all the gin mills in the world . . . etc."

"Joannie, I'm home. What's for dinner?" had joined the

gallery of the immortals. "Have a piece fruit, State Senator." To hell with it! I was a star!

Between *I Married Joan* and *Gilligan's Island*, I made one picture after another. I've lost count, but among them were *The Great Lover* and *Critic's Choice* with Bob Hope, *Mad, Mad, etc. World* with Spencer Tracy, *Hurry Sundown* with Jane Fonda and Michael Caine, *Ask Any Girl* with Shirley MacLaine and David Niven, *Man of a Thousand Faces* with James Cagney, *Above and Beyond* (in which I played General Curtis Le May) with Robert Taylor, *John Goldfarb, Please Come Home* with Peter Ustinov and again the brilliant Shirley MacLaine, and two legitimate plays: George Bernard Shaw's *Captain Brassbound's Conversion*, with Greer Garson, and a revival of that Thornton Wilder classic, *Our Town*, with Henry Fonda. I've had the pleasure of working with some of the finest talents of our time, but the most blazing of them all was James Dean.

Before we started the actual shooting of *Rebel Without a Cause*, Nick Ray got Jimmy and me together and we spent a lot of time discussing the relationship between the father and son and analyzed the motivation of each scene, rather than simply going over the dialogue. We studied the entire script in continuity, instead of the usual movie practice of learning isolated scenes as they come up in the shooting schedule. The picture was shot that way, too— from the beginning to the end in sequence, wherever it was economically possible.

James Dean worked very closely with Nick. May I say that this is the first time in the history of motion pictures that a twenty-four-year-old boy, with only one movie to his credit, was practically the codirector. Jimmy insisted on utter realism. And looking back, I sometimes wonder how we finished so violent a picture without someone getting seriously injured. For example, in one scene where Jimmy and another young man had a fight with switchblade knives, the knives were the real McCoy. And this is one of the few films where doubles were never used.

To digress for a moment, I'm afraid the public has a misconception about the use of doubles. The fact that actors are doubled in many hazardous stunts has long been the subject of jokes. Actually, far less doubling goes on than the TV comics have led you to believe. Most actors do as many of their stunts as the studios will permit. When the production department insists on having an actor doubled, it is only because there is so much money involved. If, let us say, an actor had to do a fight scene in the middle of the picture and got a sprained ankle or even a bruise on his face that could not be covered by makeup, this would hold up production and would cost the studio many thousands of dollars.

A great many people, including members of our craft, seem to feel that Jimmy had some sort of secret weapon or magic formula. I do not go along with this. I know that if anyone was ever dedicated to the art of acting, it was Jimmy. He had the greatest power of concentration I have ever encountered. He prepared himself so well in advance for any scene he was playing that the lines were not simply something he had memorized—they were actually a very real part of him. Before the take of any scene, he would go off by himself for five or ten minutes and think about what he had to do, to the exclusion of everything else. He returned when he felt he was enough in character to shoot the scene.

On the stage an actor has a chance to build and sustain a character, and through his evening performance, finally to reach a climax. Unfortunately, this cannot be done in motion pictures, and many times you have to plunge cold into a highly emotional scene. When this was the case, Jimmy would key himself up by vigorously jumping up and down, shadow boxing, or climbing up and down a fifty-foot ladder that ran to the top of the sound stage. (Little did he know he was "ladder rattling," a term used by old-time stage actors for this practice.)

In one scene in *Rebel*, he was brought into Juvenile Hall

on a charge of drunk and disorderly conduct. The scene called for him to have an intensely dramatic argument with the officer in charge and end up by hysterically banging on the desk in frustration and rage. Before the actual filming of the scene, he kept the cast and crew waiting for one whole hour. Keeping an entire company waiting for an hour sent the production department into a panic. I overheard one old crew member say, "What the hell does he think he's doing? Even Garbo never got away with that."

Jimmy spent the hour preparing for his scene, sitting in his darkened dressing room with a record player blasting out the "Ride of the Valkyrie," and drinking a quart of cheap red wine. When he felt ready, he stormed out, strode onto the set, did the scene, which was practically a seven-minute monologue, in one take, so brilliantly that even the hard-boiled crew cheered and applauded. He played that scene so intensely that he broke two small bones in his hand when he beat on the desk, which he practically demolished. Actually, he saved the production department money with his method of making them wait while he prepared himself for his one-take perfection. As a matter of fact, on the average "A" picture, seven minutes of film is considered a pretty fine full day's work.

The crucial scene in *Rebel* comes when Jimmy and I have a terrible argument at the top of a staircase, at the climax of which he throws me down the flight of stairs, across the living room, into a chair which goes over backward, and he tries to choke me to death. There is only one way to do such a scene. I had to remain completely passive and put my trust in Jimmy. If I, for any reason, got tense, we both could have been severely injured or even killed.

I was 200 pounds of dead weight, and this boy, who could not have weighed more than 140, tossed, carried, dragged, and lifted me down those stairs, across the room, and into the chair over and over again all day long, while they shot their many angles.

Due to the tremendous intensity with which Jimmy Dean

approached his work, people got the impression that he was rude, ill-tempered, and surly. At first, I must admit, I felt the same way about him. After I got to know him, I realized that he was very shy, although essentially a very warm person.

I was one of the few people who knew what his real ambition was. He secretly wanted to be a baggy-pants comedian and was quietly working on a nightclub act. Believe me, he would have "killed" the people.

I never will forget the night when Henny and I were driving along in the car, listening to the radio, and the shock with which we heard the news flash of his untimely death. To this day, we can't believe that the vital, talented James Dean is gone. The entertainment world had lost the greatest young actor of our time, and I had lost a friend.

Gilligan's Island

I was having breakfast on the veranda of the Hanalei Plantation. The view was spectacular—the mountains, the aquamarine sea, and in the distance, wreathed in fog, Bali Hai. The real Bali Hai. This was where they filmed *South Pacific*. They turned the hotel into the plantation of Emile de Beck, and right now for ten bucks you could get a platoon of Polynesian kiddies to serenade you with ten or fifteen choruses of "Happy Talk." I guess for a price you could even get Mary Martin to sing it. I had been here for only ten days and already I had succumbed to the blandishments of the islands. I caught myself referring to back home as "the mainland." I called all people "wahinis," and when in doubt I said, "Aloha." "Aloha" can mean anything—"Hello," "Good-bye," "Get me a corned beef sandwich"—anything.

The breakfast was really very aloha. Fried eggs on pineapple. I glanced at my watch. Seven A.M. I had more than half an hour before they came to take me to the actual location. The location was a closely guarded secret. I had a late work call. By late call they meant eight A.M., which in turn meant six A.M. wake-up, and "be showered and shaved and have had breakfast," the memo said. If the production man felt in a particularly jocular mood, the call would read, "having had breakfast and thrown up." Oddly enough, all production men use that line. It seems to be a tradition, like the initials M.O.S., which is sometimes necessary and means "mit out sound."

I was taking my first sip of the strong Hawaiian coffee when I saw the second assistant director of this pilot scurrying up the walk. I could tell he was the second assistant—they're always in a hysterical hurry, consulting their clipboard as they go, through dark shades which is *de rigueur* for a second assistant director on location, be it in the Belgian Congo or Point Barrow, Alaska.

Let me give you the chain of command on any self-respecting TV shoot. First there is the executive producer, then the producer, then the associate producer, so called because he is the only one who can associate with the producer. Then we come to the meat and potatoes, the nuts and bolts, the first assistant director, who is the equivalent of a First Sergeant in the army. He dumps everything on the second assistant, particularly the chore of calling the actors to the set, which is an odious task at best. Seeing me, he said, "Take your time, Mr. Backus. I've got to collect Natalie Schafer and see that she brings her lorgnette and her parasol. We'll stop on the way back and pick you up in the station wagon."

"How's it going?" I asked the hyperventilating second assistant.

"Christ awful! Some Seventh-day Adventists on a tour found our set! By the way, sir, my name is Norman. Anything I can do for you, let me know," he said, eyeing a succulent body makeup lady in a low-cut Albert Schweitzer jungle suit.

"Thank you, Norman. Oh, by the way, have they finally decided what they're going to call this little epic?"

Norman flicked through a sheaf of papers and looked up. "Yes, *Gilligan's Island*."

"Gilligan's Island?" I asked.

Norman shrugged as if to say, "Don't blame me!" and scuttled away like a startled crab.

I am sure each of us of a certain age knows where he was when he first heard the news of the bombing of Pearl Harbor, F.D.R.'s death, and the assassination of President John F. Kennedy. I heard the appalling news of the slaying of our young President on my way to location over the crackling radio in a termite-ridden station wagon. I shall certainly never forget that morning on the beach trying to play comedy, trying to get the lines out, to be funny, to do what the script demanded, to keep back the tears, to get the lines out and not hold up production.

There we were in our character wardrobes, Tina Louise in a shimmering evening gown; Alan Hale, the Skipper, in his proper seagoing attire; Dawn Wells as Mary Ann in her gingham shorts; Russell Johnson, the Professor, in his left-wing tweeds; Lovey Howell with her parasol and lorgnette and the poodle of the month under her arm; me as Thurston Howell in my Palm Beach mufti, scanning the horizon with a pair of binoculars that would have made Bull Halsey pale with envy; and, of course, Bobby Denver in his sailor suit, as the hapless, not-too-bright star named Gilligan. This was to have been the best day of all, wrap day of our pilot, with the inevitable party to follow. It was all we could do to get through it and stagger back to our hotel rooms to pack, in the hope of getting a plane for home as soon as possible.

I remember that news was hard to come by. There were rumors floating by all day. Lyndon Johnson had been killed! The Supreme Court was running the country! Castro had stormed the beaches of Florida! . . . The people in Honolulu kept looking back over their shoulders because, after all, Pearl Harbor was still fresh in their minds.

Once in Honolulu, the Navy invited us aboard one of their aircraft carriers. The deck of the carrier was bigger than a football field. The jets flew over in formation, its lead plane missing, followed by taps over the S.S. *Arizona*. I remember the twenty-one-gun salute, and I remember the tears.

Three months later I was on the "red eye" bound for New York, where I was to do a special of *Damn Yankees*. I battened myself down prior to takeoff when someone with the right number of "excuse me's" clambered over me to the window seat that the stewardess had assured me would be mine once we were airborne. I recognized my unwelcome seatmate as the powerful network head known to us all as "the Smiling Cobra." Having met before, we exchanged amenities, and I accepted an illicit pre-takeoff martini he so kindly gave me from his silver flask. I glanced around the plane and noticed that there were a number of high-level network executives, a few giants from the agent world, and some independent producers, or packagers as they are now called, each with a closely held can of film under his arm. It dawned on me that this was "selling season," the time of year when people with a pilot film would have a chance to submit it to the networks in hopes of getting into the schedule for the fall season.

"Where did we first meet?" asked my seatmate, suddenly rising. "Oh, yes, I remember," he added, stretching, "the club. Golf, right?"

"Right," I nodded, thinking to myself, This is not the best time to be talking to him.

"What the hell are you going to New York for?" he asked, as he seated himself once more. "Gonna help them peddle that *Gilligan's Island* turkey you made?"

I must have looked stricken as he continued.

"Now, mind you, I don't blame you. That rich guy you play kills me, but that film you made is the worst piece of garbage I've ever seen. Stuck on a desert island? Come on now! I'm sorry, Jim," he said, as he smiled his cobra smile.

I looked around the plane for our writer-producer Sherwood Schwartz to bail me out.

"Sherwood's a good writer," the great executive added.
"Good credits. But he must have needed some fast F.Y.
money. He knows our policy this year. No stranded-on-a-
desert-island or beached-whale stories. I know he knew
because I told him when he was in my office. I gave him
some advance money for a script and an option for thirteen
more—complete freedom—cast to be submitted for our
approval, then go ahead, make the pilot."

The best I could manage was a sickly smile. Oh, to be
up front where the execs were having themselves a little
crap game.

"Then," he continued, "he shows up with this abomi-
nation. If there was a way to sue and get my money back,
I'd do it!" The great man paused. "You know how many
'stranded' scripts I get a month? And all by accredited
writers—Simon, Burrows, Uris—they've all got a desert
island in their repertoire. *Swiss Family Robinson?* Hell, I
turned that one down. *The Admirable Crichton*—an English family on a desert island. The only one who can cope
is the butler, Crichton. Awful! What the hell am I telling
you all this for?"

"But our story is not on a desert island," I interrupted
him weakly. "It's a jungle island."

The Smiling Cobra glared. "Desert, jungle, same thing,
except one has trees. You want to do something on a de-
serted island? I'll give you an idea for free. You and that
new comic that's causing so much smoke—black fellow,
what's his name?"

"Cosby," I volunteered.

"That's the one. Was in my office last week. I told him,
change your name. Too much like Bing's. Now, I'd put
you and him on a desert island—like Crusoe and his man
Friday. Oh, and they're both just divorced, and one's neat
and the other one's a slob. Think about that!"

The great executive turned off the light, coiled himself up, and, with a smile of innocence on his face, was instantly asleep.

In their seats along the aisles, as if on cue, the mastodons of the media closed their bloodshot eyes, and I swear I heard softly wafting through the plane, "Good night, David." "Good night, Chet," as the huge silver crib in the sky hurtled itself toward the Big Apple.

Tuesday morning at nine o'clock. I was finishing my breakfast in the Oak Room of the Plaza and studying my already dog-eared script when I was interrupted by a cheery, "Good morning, Jim." I looked up and saw David Gerber, a young, enterprising agent who was destined for much bigger things. He sat down.

"Hey, Jim, haven't you heard? *Gilligan's Island* is in!"

"C'mon, Dave," I said. "That doesn't make sense. Sunday night I was on the 'red eye' seated next to the Cobra, and he said *Gilligan's Island* was a piece of garbage and he was contemplating suing Sherwood."

"Well, cheer up," said Dave. "It's probably just a rumor, anyway."

He spotted another of his colleagues and ran off to cluster-spread the news.

I motioned the waiter for a phone and called Henny, who was on her way to the pool.

"It's true!" she said. "They just phoned from CBS."

The next thing I heard was a splash. The operator cut in. "There's a call waiting."

"Put it through."

I was greeted by the most confident, positive-thinking man I have ever known. It was Mr. Schwartz, the Mary Poppins of Sherwood Forest, and his happy voice.

"We're on!" he said, and it was true, as your children and grandchildren can attest. *Gilligan's Island* had made the schedule, to be shown every Saturday night at 8:30.

How it ever got on the schedule no one has ever been able to explain satisfactorily. This is the most plausible explanation, and the one I believe. It has to do with that old bone of contention: should there or shouldn't there be a laugh track on a comedy show? Personally, I feel that it is next to impossible to play comedy without an audience, but it just won't work if they get an honest track and then jazz it up.

I remember back in the Stone Age, on *I Married Joan*, we used a track even then. We would hire a screening room and corral 250 or so misbegotten souls for our audience. I would come out and introduce myself, then bring on Joan and the rest of the members of the cast. I'd tell a few jokes, put on the film and tape their reactions. That, in a nutshell, is all that's ever needed. Not those hyped-up improvements those eager beavers sometimes add.

During the days of *Gilligan*—and I gather this is still true—for the pilot of any new film they test the reactions by showing it to an audience they gather (preferably those wearing Bermuda shorts and carrying a camera) at the Preview House. This is a 300-seat theatre that is completely wired with buttons to push.

"Would you watch this show every week?"

"What did you like best?"

"Did anything offend you?"

"Is the show funny?"

"Would you let your children watch it?"

Before they run the pilot, to test the level of the audience's responses and laughter, they run a *Mr. Magoo* to get what they consider the perfect reactions.

By some fluke, by mistake, by chicanery, who knows, *Gilligan's Island* was included in the lineup of shows to be tested. And our little tropical island fantasy went right through the roof. So Cobra or no Cobra, they had to put it on, or, thanks to the TV scuttlebutt, one of the other networks would have grabbed it.

Some three years later I was in New York to do a one-night stand. I was having lunch at the Regency and was still groggy from no sleep. And, like the desperate fool that I am, I had taken a sleeping pill at six o'clock A.M. Remind me to personally maim, kill, and obliterate my agent. I remember three years ago when he said I didn't have to sing in *Damn Yankees*. I remember him saying, in essence, "I can get you 'favored nations'* with Lee Remick and Phil Silvers, plus expenses, first class all the way. Don't I always protect my pussycat? It'll be stealing money. You play the captain of the Yankees baseball team." I said, "Wait a minute. Doesn't the captain have to sing? I'm no singer. You know that."

"Sing? No, lover," laughed Al. "He's in the dugout with all the great lines. You yell them at the guys out in the field. A wonderful part!"

So what happens? I show up for the first reading and who do you think it turns out has the hit number? That's right, me! "You Gotta Have Heart," no less. What's more, first I sing it alone. Then I'm joined in the song by the team, every one of whom is a Broadway-trained singer-dancer-actor. I said to the producer at the first reading, "Listen, Mr. Divine, I'm no singer."

"Don't worry," he told me. "When Hal gets through with you, you'll sing."

Hal Hastings was the veteran conductor of some twenty-five Broadway musicals. Said Hal, "You'll sing if I have to rehearse you twenty-four hours a day."

And we did.

So here I was some three selling seasons later, having lunch at the Regency Hotel in New York City, hoping the eggs Benedict would take care of the jet lag. I was booked in for just one night. As Al so succinctly put it, "It's a license to steal, bubbie! Would I lie to you?! It's just a little dinner at the Waldorf. Some big insurance company or something, who knows? Who cares? As long as we get that certified check. Right? All you have to do is introduce

---

*Favored nations: Each star to receive the same salary. (Gee! I thought it was an agreement between two or more banana republics!)

Diahann Carroll. Oh, maybe do—ten or fifteen minutes or so—"

I started to sputter. He jumped in.

"Then you get on the 'red eye' and grab a little shut-eye."

"But listen, Al, I haven't had a chance to write any material. I haven't—"

He cut me off.

"Look, sweetie, all you have to do is tell a few little jokes and introduce her, then grab that one A.M. job on TWA and it's home and mother. How sweet it is!"

"That's a lousy imitation of Jackie Gleason," I said desperately, still trying to think of some way to weasel out.

"Oh, that reminds me, you don't mind if the driver picks you up in the lobby at seven-thirty? I know that's a little early, but he has to pick up Gleason at Newark Airport. He's coming in from Florida."

"I thought you said this was just a little party some insurance people were—" I was sputtering again.

"It's just you and Jackie and Diahann," he assured me. "I don't know how Don Rickles and Jack Carter will ever get there. Let their agents worry," he added blithely.

I was beside myself. "Listen, Al!" I shouted.

"Bubbie, don't get hysterical. You have to do a show! *Calm down*! You just come on right after intermission. A little fifteen-minute intermission."

(I knew these intermissions. Only half the audience comes back, and the rest have had a few.)

"Then the limo will rush you to JFK," he continued. "Don't even worry about dinner. You can grab a nice little midnight snack on the plane. Like I said, it's just like stealing money. Nice little package, if I do say so myself."

"I've seen better packages at Safeway," I grumbled.

"Funny! Funny! Mind if I give that to Berle? He can use it on the show."

"Don't tell me Milton's going to be there, too!"

"Just five fast minutes! That's all he's gonna do, and

that's before the invocation. Oh, didn't I tell you? They were lucky! They got Monsignor Sheen. Well, after all, he's just across the street at Saint Pat's, and—"

"I'll be there," I yelled. I hung up. What's the use, I thought. I had learned long ago that as a client of Al's you can't win. Actually, in the long run he was on the button—that is, if you lived long enough. Anyway, he was the best we had.

I took a sip of my coffee and tried to forget all about why I was in New York. Suddenly I remembered that CBS had set up an interview for me at noon with one of New York's top columnists, Earl Wilson. And there he was, standing in the doorway. He spotted me and made his way to my table.

He sat down, and I ordered him some coffee. Earl, a top Broadway scribe, wrote his column from the viewpoint of a country bumpkin who believed that life backstage was slightly naughty. Since he, too, was from Ohio, that took care of the openers—news and regards from fellow Ohioans Bob Hope, Phyllis Diller, Hugh Downs, Jack Paar, and Jonathan Winters, to name a few. For some reason, Ohio was a breeding ground for comedians, the same way Philadelphia spawned so many Italian boy singers. Could it be the water? Of course, with New York comics it's the seltzer!

As we were chatting away about Ohio, a waiter interrupted.

"Telephone call for you, Mr. Backus. Long distance," he said, as he plugged in the phone. "It's a Mr. Schwartz."

It was always good to hear from Mary Poppins. I happily picked it up.

"Sherwood!"

"Hey, Jim! We're picked up! Henny told me where you were. We're picked up for a fourth season!" He was jubilant.

"Of course we're picked up, Sherwood. Why wouldn't we be picked up? We're never out of the top ten. I never doubted it for a minute. Don't you look at the numbers?"

"Well," said Sherwood, sounding slightly deflated. "I thought you'd like to hear it from me."

"I'm thrilled, Sherwood," I assured him. "It was nice of you to call. Let's celebrate Saturday night, when I get back."

"Great! It's a date."

We hung up. Earl leaned in. "I heard that. Congratulations! Tell you what I'm gonna do. I'm going to devote this whole column to just *Gilligan's Island*. My boy, Slugger, watches it. He got me hooked. I kinda like it. Now, about Tina Louise, what's her bust measurement?"

"How the hell do I know?!" I exploded. "What difference does it make? Make it up."

"It's important!" he said seriously. "I always give the bust measurements—you know *that* if you read my column. It's the first thing I always ask them. I've got a file full of bust measurements of ladies I've interviewed. Some of the most famous women in the world!"

"You must have been a big hit with Eleanor Roosevelt!" I laughed.

"I know how to get Tina's measurements," he said. "I'll call Howard Hughes."

He checked it off on his pad. "C'mon, Jim, how about Tina Louise?"

I sighed. "Earl, Tina is a fooler. She's into a lot of things. Psychoanalysis, astrology, Science of the Mind, Buddhism. She's a serious acting student. Studies at the Actors Studio with Lee Strasberg. Last year she quietly married Les Crane, who was then the host of a talk show. She got the entire cast of *Gilligan's* to give her away. Garden wedding, Sunday afternoon, flower girls, ring bearer, the seven of us behind the bride and groom on the 'I do's.' Then all the classic wedding schtick, the getaway car, the old shoes, the sign that said, JUST MARRIED, the confetti. We're the only show in prime time with rice marks."

"Oh, that's good, Jim, that's good! I'll use it!" he said, taking it all down with his stubby pencil. "The Professor,

how about the Professor, Mr. Know-Everything? Is he like
that off-screen, too?"

"Oh, come on, Earl. That's Russ Johnson. And he does
know everything. It's darn good casting. A very well-
educated gentleman and one of the nicest guys I've ever
worked with. What's more important, he's a hell of an
actor."

He wrote a few words and looked up eagerly. "Mary Ann.
What about her? That's Slugger's favorite. I hear she's a
beauty contest winner."

"How old is Slugger?" I asked, signaling for more coffee.

"Fourteen," he told me.

"Figures. Her name is Dawn Wells. She comes from the
Wells Fargo family. And she *is* a beauty contest winner.
Miss Nevada. She's never out of those gingham short shorts.
Miss Laughing Bottom, we call her. She's another hard-
working actress. Studies everything. Very ambitious."

He looked up. "Okay. Mrs. Howell?"

"Lovey?" I grinned. "Oh, you know her, Earl. That's
Natalie Schafer, from the theatre."

"Sure I know her, but what's she like?"

"Pure New York theatre. 'Jim's other wife,' Henny calls
her. They're great friends. She's as vague in real life as she
is on the box. Flighty as a tipsy butterfly. But don't worry
about Natalie, she's putting the world on! She's blind as a
bat. Those lorgnettes are on the level. She's a lousy driver,
too, but she insists on driving herself. I said, 'Natalie, get
a limo. You can afford it. You know, you can't take it with
you.' She looked at me through those glasses on a stick
and said, 'Jimmy, if I can't take it with me, I won't go!'
She comes from a rich family," I kidded. "They made their
money the hard way, they stole it."

"Oh," said Earl, scribbling away. "That's a great joke.
I'll be sure to use it. Now, the big question. Gilligan and
the Skipper. Is it true they're a little light-footed?"

"That's ridiculous!" I laughed. "They have the same relationship as any captain and his cabin boy. Anyway, they're both happily married. Alan Hale, the Skipper, is a Hollywood brat. His father was a big star in the thirties and forties. Alan mother-hens us, cooks for us at least once a week. Moonlights in his own restaurant on La Cienega Boulevard. Bobby Denver, Gilligan, is a former schoolteacher—taught fourth grade. Had to become an actor, with all that talent. How could he miss? He can't do anything wrong. Carries the whole show on those skinny little shoulders. He really has no idea how good he is. We all call him the Saint Francis of Assisi of Studio City! Has a ranch in Hawaii and one out West. Crazy about animals, which he houses in his dressing room—no one in his right mind would dare go in there! God knows what scaly or furry friend he has sharing his digs. He's so hung up on animals he once took an eight-hundred-pound gorilla back home with him in a roomette. Even took him into the dining car," I told Earl kiddingly.

"He did? Where did he sit?"

"Any damn place he wanted to! Bobby also has a couple of porcupines—but that's another story. . . .

"You know, Earl, we have a marvelous cast and, amazingly enough, although we've been together a lot of years, I swear to you we've never had a cross word."

Earl leafed through his notes. "Now, about you—"

"Oh, come on, Earl, just go through your files."

With that, he gathered up his papers and rose. "Well," he said, "this is tomorrow's column. Thanks, Jim. Give Henny my best, and love from Rosemary."

He headed for the door as I toasted him with the centerpiece.

Another endless evening! But it was over! I did it—the show! Oh, thanks a lot, Al! When would I ever learn? What the hell, it was a good day, anyway. We were picked up. I fully expected it, but in our business anything can happen.

There was just enough time to get back to the Regency and change into something loose for the ride home.

It was getting late now. I had changed, made a few phone calls, and was downstairs signing my bill when Frank, the concierge, handed me the phone. It was Earl Wilson.

"Hey, Jim! Get this! You're canceled! How about that? It just came over the wire! What a great tag for my column! Listen, when you find out what really happened, give me a ring, will you? I'll do another column on the show. Great, huh? Say hello to Henny!"

He hung up. I hadn't said a goddamn word. I was speechless. Nice of him to call before the flight to give me the good news—I needed that.

Months later, after rumors and sagas and Eddas, we pieced it all together.

It seems . . .

In rearranging the fall schedule, word came down from the tower that the demographics* showed that the network was topheavy with folksy comedy. *Gilligan's Island* was hardly *Private Lives*, but we must have been doing something right, since we continuously beat out our competition and, what's more, we were cheap—I mean, inexpensive.

Now what happened was, CBS had finally canceled that long-running western, *Gunsmoke.* The screams of protest from irate viewers resounded from across the nation.

"Remove *Gunsmoke?* Would you kick a dog named Spot?"

"Remove *Gunsmoke?* Would you paint mustaches on Mount Rushmore?"

"Remove *Gunsmoke?* Would you spit on Old Glory?"

So back it went into the lineup. But where to put it? *Gunsmoke* was a one-hour show, and there was now only

*Demographics: Breaking down a show according to audience appeal, income, age group, church affiliation, and sexual preference—if any. "Forty-eight percent of the TV viewing public goes to the bathroom during the commercials." (This is an independent lavatory test!)

one empty half-hour dangling from the schedule. It came down to this. One of these had to go, *Gilligan's Island* or *The Lucy Show*. Need I say more?

Case dismissed!

Everybody in the bus!

Cut to the owl!

In those days, according to the Screen Actors Guild, rerun residuals were granted in diminishing amounts as follows:

1st Run	Salary
2nd Run	40 percent of scale
3rd Run	30 percent of scale
4th/5th/6th Run	25 percent of scale

And that's it—that's all, folks!

This was, of course, before the days of the big TV money. I guess I was born too early or too late. When the powers that be came to us to attempt to buy us out for future replays, they started their bargaining by telling us that first of all, *Gilligan's* had been on the air for only a measly three years and didn't have enough shows to make it count for much, and furthermore, the first season of our little epic was shot in black-and-white, which would have no resale value whatsoever, as the syndicators were buying only color. They conned us, convinced us, and bought us out for a comparatively small flat sum on a "favored nations" basis. When it was finally put on the air in rerun, *Gilligan's Island* took off and, color or no color, it was and still is the most replayed comedy show in the history of television. It is playing as we speak, in just about every language, as often as five times a day in some markets. In Los Angeles alone, on weekends, it has been on the tube back to back. As Rudyard Kipling might have said, "The sun never sets on *Gilligan's Island*."

So how much do the seven castaways get from all this?

Nada.

    Eppis.

        Nichts.

            Niente.

                Bubkis.

As for me, I cry a lot.

Stage Fright

After *Gilligan's Island* came years of movies, TV, benefits, clubs, Las Vegas, commercials, specials, a one-man show. Pressure, pressure, pressure. Total insanity, and—finally —a crackup.

During the past six years I have been poked and prodded by some of the finest medical mavens on the West Coast. They are still trying to diagnose my arcane malady. Their evaluations have all been variations on a theme—"Minimal Parkinson's Disease" (it's no worse than a bad cold) . . . "malfunctioning Basal Ganglia"* (you die with it, not from it). But nothing about that excruciating pain at the end of my tailbone (where the sun don't shine). For this they had no opinions. But when it was G.L.'s turn, my wise old psychoanalyst came up with "weaver's bottom"! That's what they really call it. Spurs on your tailbone are known to their trade as "weaver's bottom." They all agreed for the hundredth time that maybe 5 percent of it was organic; the rest was caused by my super hypochondria. They went

*Basal Ganglia: A nerve of the motor system that transmits messages from the brain to other ganglia—a malfunction that causes the patient to do bad imitations of Jerry Lewis. (From the Latin *ganglia-banglia*.)

190

around and around on that one, and for some reason they reminded me of the stagehands who gave me my early sexual education. Those union label buddhas who dozed their life away in the half-light of theatres claimed that masturbating will cause hair to grow on the palms of your hands, that we human beings have only so many orgasms in us and once that number is reached, that's it! Forget it!

I first heard all this when I was a sixteen-year-old kid hanging around backstage at the Cleveland Playhouse. I remember every word they told me, which just goes to prove that the stagehands were also right when they said that when you reach the Golden Years, although you can't remember what happened yesterday, your memory becomes a veritable laser beam into the distant past.

The voice of G.L. brought me back to the present. I was still standing there in my shorts before that medical panel who were still trying to find out what the hell was wrong with me. It was wily old G.L. who finally came up with it.

"Stage fright!" was all he said.

Stage fright? Stage fright in my profession was like hiccups to a glass blower, a hernia to a weight lifter! My God! It's like vertigo to a steeplejack! Was that what this was all about?

"Yezzir," they all echoed, "that's what it is!"

"You're right, G.L. It's a giant case of stage fright!"

They congratulated G.L. and left, delighted to have solved this annoying problem. But where did that leave me?

Could it be? Stage fright usually strikes without warning and, God knows, without reason. It hit Lord Laurence Olivier when he was in his sixties. He knew if he gave in to it he would never act again. Through a mental quirk, he discovered that he could get through a performance only if a certain friend of his, a man who had nothing whatever to do with the play, stood in the wings directly in his sight line while he performed. It was crazy, but it worked.

Stage fright is not merely confined to the stage. It strikes toilers in every medium of show business. All of us are vulnerable. Burt Reynolds is a movie actor. He hyperventilates. To gain relief from this little manifestation, you have to breathe into a paper bag. You put a brown paper bag over your head and breathe. It works! Be sure you empty it first, though, or you'll have kale growing out of your ears. Don't try it with a plastic bag!

I speak for all my comrades when I say that most of us have had or will have stage fright, at least to some degree.

Pick up any magazine today and you're sure to find an article by a noted psychiatrist on stress anxiety, agoraphobia, hyperventilation—whatever. All of those and more are under the "stage fright" umbrella. The symptoms are the same—dry mouth, loss of balance, heart palpitations and, worst of all of course, the accompanying fear of dying.

In the legitimate theatre stage fright is with you about twenty-three hours a day. It leaves you for an hour or two after the curtain comes down, while you're still up on the ceiling with the applause ringing in your ears. But back it creeps to that little corner of your brain and there it stays until the curtain descends the next night.

The theatres themselves do not exactly help the situation. Backstage, with very rare exceptions, has all the ambience of Devil's Island. As for those dressing rooms! Talk about no frills! They're usually cramped, stark, airless, and uncomfortable. They generally contain two identical chairs—one for your agent?—both with raveled cane bottoms. And once you are safely impaled there, a bronze-lunged youth flings open the door to intone, "Half hour!" I know it's half hour. There's no need to threaten me! They don't do that at IBM or J. Walter Thompson or even Smith Barney. They assume you are reasonably intelligent and know you are supposed to be on the job. Then, when your heart gets back to normal, the same brassy voice—like a proclamation of doom—calls, "Fifteen minutes!" We also know when it's fifteen minutes. We all know it's getting close to the moment of truth. Why rub it in? We don't need a greeter from Forest Lawn caressing our nerves with emory paper. Now that this harbinger of doom has reduced us to frightened newts, he says, "Five minutes, please!" Note this time he adds "please." Why not? On Death Row you get a steak dinner. That five-minute call comes just in time for a last-minute trip to the loo—just for insurance. What the hell, you never can tell. Just my luck, on my last opening night the iron door jammed. Then I really had to go! I tried to kick it open, but at that moment the boy with the Klaxon horn voice yelled, "Places, please! On stage, everybody!" Too late. Nothing like playing the first act with a busted toe and a full bladder!

No one medium has ever had a lock on stage fright. Each has its own particular terrifying aspects, but the winner hands down—and I'm sure my fellow actors will agree—was the live TV dramas emanating from New York: *Kraft Theatre*, *Robert Montgomery Presents*, *Westinghouse Playhouse*, *U. S. Steel Hour*, and *Playhouse Ninety*, to name but a few. They had one thing in common, that chilling word, "L I V E!" It was happening right before your eyes, at that moment—no retakes, no second chance. And for those dedicated actors probing in a new medium, no cue cards—and no idiot boards.

Late in the summer of 1958, I was brought East to play the lead in a *Kraft Theatre*. So, being a novice in live TV, I was apprehensive, to say the least. I couldn't help recalling stories I had heard. Like the one about the poor actor who was playing a scene in an airplane set who went blank out of sheer panic and said, "Well, this is where I get off"— and stepped out of his window seat at 30,000 feet! Or that old character man I ran into at that time, whom I asked, "What in God's name do you do if you go up in your lines?" He replied sagely, "Well, when I go up, I keep right on moving my lips. That way people think their sound has gone off."

Well, here I was, about to play the lead in an hour-long live television show. The piece concerned a boarding-house full of losers. I was to be a frustrated novelist who was forced to earn his living by writing trash for pulp magazines. The inmates of this unfortunate establishment came to him with their problems, frustrations, and broken dreams. He in turn tried to help them, but at the same time made use of them in his writings. As he wrote, I—as the novelist—acted out their fantasies. These involved my portraying a Nebraska dirt farmer, a Greek sea captain, a Nazi tank commander, an alcoholic carnival barker, and a defrocked Jesuit priest. All very mystic, all very Rod Serling with overtones of Paddy Chayevsky. It was an urban purgatory.

Why I took the part I'll never know. There were five changes, two with alternate makeups. Now, mind you, this was live, and two minutes for a change was a luxury. On one of my changes there was no time to leave the stage at all, so they kept the camera tight on my face, while down below there were three or four wardrobe people changing me from the skin out.

The part was longer than *King Lear*, and we had only two weeks for rehearsal. The director was one of the wunderkinder who had sprung into prominence in those few short years—Bogart, Felton, Lafferty, and Lumet, to name a few. He was inspired and sympathetic and tried to make me feel comfortable, but there was a feeling of rivalry between the cast and myself. I was lumped into that category of "Coast actor," one who had sold out and spent his days cruising the Sunset Strip in a Bentley convertible between pictures with endless shooting schedules and exotic locations. They, on the other hand, were "New York actors," ferociously talented, members of the Actors Studio—dedicated artists who lived in lofts on the Lower East Side, who came to rehearsal on motor scooters—leather clad—with a girl riding on the rear fender with whom they were having a relationship, which was made possible by group therapy. In limbo were some English character men, militantly pukkah, who referred to the United States as the "Colonies" and who toasted the Queen in their sleazy Broadway fleabags when the sun went over the yardarm. They were the type of English character actor who had played everything from musicals to Shakespeare—all of it in the provinces. The sort that tell each other tales like:

ACTOR 1: Do you think Hamlet slept with his mother?

ACTOR 2: He did in every company I ever toured with!

Once we waded through each other's bullshit and got down to business, the rehearsals went swimmingly, and acting once again was fun.

"Five minutes till air!" The voice had the grim anonymity of a railroad station announcer. The two weeks of rehearsing in a ballroom over a kosher delicatessen on New York's Lower East Side were finished. The last three days had been spent in an old Upper East Side movie theatre that had been converted into a television studio. Now we had the sets, the props, the wardrobe, and the makeup, with which we did run-through after run-through, nonstop run-throughs with the actual show timing, and with all the split-second changes, after which came notes with the director.

One note that I will never forget was when I was playing in *Our Town*. In this Thornton Wilder classic, everything is pantomimed. There are no sets, no props, nothing. Just the bare stage. After our first run-through we assembled around our director, Henry Fonda. I can still hear that Nebraska twang. "Jim, it's almost right, but in that scene with the milkman, when you said, 'Good morning,' you walked through his horse."

So I tried to listen to this new young director. Small intrusions kept nagging my mind like a crazed kaleidescope, two and three of them at once. Ads from when I was a kid, aimed at the all-American boy, were filtering through: "Old Town Canoes! . . . Win a canoe! . . . Earn big money!" "Be a Postal Clerk!" "Find the faces in the trees and win a bicycle!" Oh, calm down! Pay attention! The play! The play's the thing with which we'll catch the conscience of the king. "Earn big money, be a king!"

The cast, in the greenroom, waiting to go on, all had little rituals to help them prepare. The "leather jackets" with the girls on the back of the bike were all involved with their "method" exercises—a lot of grunting and muffled primal screams. One of the Actors Studio actresses was off in a corner running in place with her arms extended and hands hanging down limp like wet noodles. Another was sitting on the floor in the lotus position, slowly rotating her head. Don't knock it! They had something to hang on to—Lee Strasberg! I only had God!

I could feel the panic rising in my body. I walked out onto the stage. I'd better sit down. It's pitch-black in here. I felt around for a chair. Nothing! At least in the theatre, unless there is a blackout, it's only semidark. There's always a light-spill from the set, or at least one strategically placed work light. But this was TV. Live TV! The more you complained about things the more they reminded you that this was the future. Then I remembered my years in radio. How easy it was. All we had to do was read off a piece of paper.

"I have a lady in the balcony, Doctor!"

"Lucky Strike Green has gone to war!"

"Right with Eversharp!"

"Call for Philip Morris!"

"Ah, there's good news tonight."

" 'Life Can Be Life!' The true-to-life story of a life that is life. "Life Can Be Life!' "

I loved it. It was a license to steal.

Even though it was almost air time, someone making a security check opened one of the side doors. I took a deep breath and peeked out. It was a lovely summer twilight. I caught a glimpse of a sidewalk café. Attractive young people were having cocktails across the narrow little street. I could hear the tinkle of ice in their glasses and their laughter. Damn them! What the hell was I doing here, anyway? It wasn't fair. Me, about to go on—live—for an hour.

They shut the door. God, it was dark in here. Darker than ever now. Dark as a well-digger's ass. No, that's as *cold* as a well-digger's ass. No, that's cold as a witch's tit. No, she got them caught in a wringer. What am I thinking about! I must be going nuts. . . . What are my lines? Oh, God, I can't remember my lines! What's my first line? Oh, stop shaking, you fool. In a minute you have to hold up a bottle of milk and then pour it into a glass. . . .

Suddenly, like a clap of thunder, a searing white light went through my brain. What if I didn't go on? What would happen? What could they do to me? Why should I go on? "The show must go on"? Who says so? The producer? My agent? "It'll up your income," he said. Up his! And up his 10 percent! I could just sneak out that side door and maybe join that group at the sidewalk café. Could they sue me? Bar me from ever working again? Maybe I could get run over a little bit . . . that would show them!

The voice suddenly roared, "Ten, nine, eight, seven, six . . ."

I was numb.

"Five, four . . ."

Oh, God, what's the first line?

"Three, two . . ."

The fickle finger of fate pointed—and I was on.

Early the next morning I was nestled in the iron womb of a brand-new DC 7, comfortably on my way in the new nonstop seven-hour flight to L.A. The stewardess had just handed me a glass of champagne and the New York papers, which I practically snatched out of her hand. Like a madman I turned to the television section. Ah, there it was—*Baubles in the Basement.*

"Good TV fare."

My eye ran down the page. "Jim Backus." There it was.

Jim Backus played the part of the confessor with simple charm. He went a little overboard with some of the fantasy scenes, but what a relief not to have him resort to his *Mr. Magoo* laugh. Especially effective was his entrance at the top of the show, where he came on and just stared into the camera. All the misery and panic of those tortured people yet to appear were mirrored in his eyes.

I gulped and took a large swallow of champagne. Wow! How about that! I could hardly wait to go back and do another one.

Backus Strikes Back

Well, there I was back in that chair again.

If President Reagan can start a sentence with "Well," I guess I can, too. I'm no grammarian, but I love words. Love the roll of good writing, the life, the jolt, the kick that a well-picked word will give to a sentence. Nevertheless, I defy you to read a paragraph from one of our modern novels without being assaulted by "dichotomy," "perks," "role model," "commitment," "supportive," "protagonist," "unilateral," and so forth.

"G.L.," I said, "I'm going to move and lie down on the couch. Tony doesn't have one, but it's better lying down. That way I don't have to stare at that damned ceramic owl with the clock in its brisket. Now all I get to stare at are those Wyatt Earp boots you wear.

"Now that you've cut down your patient load, the only time I get to see you is when Tony, my number one shrink, takes one of his endless vacations. By the way, I've missed you and your antediluvian politics. Oh, speaking of that, know what Jack Warner said when he heard about Ronnie Reagan running for President? 'No!' he screamed. 'Gregory Peck is for President. Ronnie Reagan is for Mayors!'

"Hey, you fellas have raised your prices again. I got a

memo from Charlie Goldring, my business manager, making me aware of the fact that you are now getting one-hundred-thirty-five bucks an hour. Not bad for a shrink in semiretirement! I memoed back to him that to do anything about losing G.L. would be like trying to replace Mount Rushmore. 'Listen, Charlie,' I wrote, 'what about keeping G.L. on the payroll all year long with Tony?! Then we'd be the first ménage-à-trois in psychiatric history.'

"I guess I flipped my lid too early this time, G.L.—I'm supposed to wait till Tony is back in town. This summer he's on a trip around the world. I wonder where he'll go next year. That's a joke, G.L.

"Okay, okay. Back to business. Remember when our last book came out? *Backus Strikes Back*? About my illness? The one where Norman Cousins was the role model? And George Burns wrote the Foreword? Listen, how supportive could they be? Supportive, there's that word again. . . . Anyway, the promotional head of Stein and Day, our publishing house, arranged our book tour, the best one I've ever seen. The positive attitude from everyone was unbelievable! Let me tell you, I was scared to death! I tried to hide it, but I was in a perpetual panic. As you well know, I'd been sick for four years. I was getting better, lots better, but the tour terrified me. I was getting more and more certain every day that I wasn't ready."

This Is Henny . . .

They all wanted us on their shows on the book tour. The demand for my husband was unbelievable! We were to tee off the book on its date of publication on the *Merv Griffin Show*, then *Hour Magazine*, the *Today Show*, *Donahue*, and on and on. From city to city, as many as they could cram in.

Most of the talk shows are fun. Some are agonizing and some are a joy, depending on your host. If you don't happen to be on early in the show, the wait is interminable. And nerve-racking. All the hosts on these shows have one thing they insist on. Even if you are a close personal friend, they don't want to see you before the show. When they greet you on your entrance, it is really for the first time. That way the greeting is always spontaneous. The power of these shows is unbelievable! If you have a book or a record or anything to plug, the response is incredible, and the long white-knuckle wait to "get on" is well worth it.

Our first book was launched on *This Is Your Life*, where they surprised Jim in the Pickwick Book Shop where he was innocently autographing books. I had promised him I would never put him through this, but the publisher, G. P. Putnam's Sons, said it was a guaranteed sale of two-hundred-thousand books. They kept insisting that I okay it. Finally, after they wore me down, I said yes. So how many books do you think they printed for the great occasion? Ten thousand! Period! When actors get together, they complain about their agents. When writers get together, they bitch about their publishers, most of whom have no idea that they're really in show business.

Our second book was called *What Are You Doing After the Orgy?* It was the simple story of a second honeymoon in Europe. Can you believe that in the middle sixties we were not allowed to mention our book title on network television? Jim was the host of *Talent Scouts* that season, and the word "orgy" made CBS so nervous that he was not even allowed to whisper it on his own show. As for NBC, when we went on the *Tonight Show*, Johnny Carson had to hold up our book in a plain brown wrapper! Ah, yes, we've come a long way, baby!

This Is Jim . . .

When you write a book, somehow you can never imagine finishing it. I mean actually saying "The End" . . . "Finis" . . . "Auf Wiedersehen" . . . "That's All, Folks!" When we wrote before I got sick, Henny kept the whole project together. Most of my time was spent working in television or pictures. All that activity, or pressure, seems to stimulate my synapses, so after my day's work as an actor, and after my marital amenities, Henny would show me what she had written or what she had put together from the stuff I had written the night before. We'd been doing this for so many years that I never thought about how we did it. We just did it.

We would discuss what we had written so far, what we were going to write, and how to shape it. Once we had agreed on what was needed, I would whip out my yellow pad and pencil and go to my study. Some hours later I would emerge with three or four pages of undisciplined "best of Backus." The next day, while I was toiling in the vineyards, Henny would tear it apart, switch it, cut it if necessary, and add it to the manuscript. Come to think of it, we wrote most of our books in bed. What other writing team can make that claim?

When the book was finally finished, accepted by the publisher and ready to go, then came the phone calls ... from the publisher, the agents, the business manager, the publicity people (God forbid you should double plant).* All this was taken care of by Henny.

When *Backus Strikes Back* came out in June 1984, with my basal ganglia malfunctioning, my Minimal Parkinson's Syndrome, and my panics still aboard, I could not work. I found myself sans movies or TV. Golf? Forget it! And as for the book, my portion of the entertainment had long been concluded. The rest was up to Henny. All those phone calls, the packing for the tour, the miles of arrangements Henny had to take care of. Right now I was only in the way—the same way the drone bugs the queen bee. I never

---

*Double plant: When your public relations man plants the same item about you in more than one column ... They are usually rival columnists, which only compounds the boo-boo.

did figure out what really happens, who does what to whom. All I know is the drone gets stung.

Sitting around in a bar was a definite no-no; alcohol was not compatible with the medication. I had nothing to do but stew.

I remember wandering aimlessly about the house one bright June day a week before the date of publication. We were to leave that day for the tour. I walked into the upstairs hall. There it was, the mound of luggage, all tagged and tabbed. The foldovers, the makeup kits, the pill bag, the midget typewriter, the crate with the hair supplies and the dryer, and of course, Henny's carpetbag that Mike Todd gave her from *Around the World in Eighty Days*—her good-luck bag. As I stared at this monstrous pile, I started to tremble at the thought of the hectic schedule to follow. Somewhere I had lost my center. I felt scattered. And that's about all I remember. . . .

This Is Henny . . .

He woke up in the hospital. He never talks about it. I don't think he remembers much. They kept him pretty sedated those first days. Of course the tour was canceled. Guess who made the phone call. And this after all our work, plans, and expenses—people on the house while we were to be gone, double watch by the patrol, new hot-weather wardrobes for shows and travel. (At home we seldom get out of swim wear and robes, and it had been years since we had left our perfect climate in the summertime.)

The *Merv Griffin Show*! What about that? The doctors promised us that Jim would be able to get out of the hospital and do the show by Wednesday . . . not to worry. Then he could check back in for further tests. On Wednesday, when they got him up and dressed, the drugs they had him on made him so dizzy it posed too great a danger. So guess who had to go to the show and tell the staff the good news?

204 FORGIVE US OUR DIGRESSIONS

I put on my makeup and my pretty new dress and girded my loins, whatever that means, and somehow I told them. They were not exactly all choked up.

I had done the show more times than I could remember. Merv had started me in talk shows way back in 1958 with our very first book. I love Merv. He's a great interviewer, with a special flair for bringing out the best in everyone, especially women. Also, he is without a doubt the best listener I've ever met.

But Jim and Henny Backus are one thing. Henny, alone, is another story. Jim's name and face are instantly recognized. As for me, you need a libretto. So I was not too surprised when they sent out an emergency call and got a young comic to put in our star spot—next to closing—and gave me Siberia, last one on. Well, okay, I must have been good. They asked me back ... alone! And if you don't believe me, come on over and I'll run it for you. And best of all, it sold us a ton of books!

They kept my darling in the hospital for almost two weeks. He had every test they could come up with. Was it really Parkinson's? Or did this talented actor in his panics subconsciously feign it? All the tests checked out. Just to be on the safe side, they upped his Sinemet, the Parkinson's medication. He came home in a wheelchair, with a nurse, and totally helpless. He was perfect, they said. Every test was a beauty. Oh, great! So we tenderly put Mr. Perfect into his bed and sat him up and fed him. He couldn't even use his hands.

Now the regimen began. As from scratch, exercise, exercise, exercise! He walked ... and swam ... and went to ballet class ... and had vocal lessons ... and physical therapy ... every day, all day, while I and the round-the-clock nurses, who were with us for eight months, tried to pull him out of his deep depression.

Slowly he responded. Slowly he walked, and sat down in a chair by himself, and got out of it alone, and fed himself, and used a pen, and now, with the exception of an occasional bad day, he moves like Fred Astaire. Does he have Parkinson's Disease? No one has the nerve to take him off the medication to find out. And those horrendous panics persist, with all their accompanying agonizing pain. They come when we least expect them, out of nowhere and with great ferocity. We can't go anywhere. We can't make any plans. We're not much fun anymore. We no longer have a maypole to dance around.

I watched him as he slept. Still too thin. So sweet, so vulnerable. I lay down beside him and held him tight. Maybe he would absorb my energy and respond. What are you afraid of, I thought, rising to cover him better. You who have everything. Why can't you shake it off? What happened somewhere back in your happy, lucky life? Is there something I don't know because you don't know?

Keep fighting, Sweetheart. You'll make it back! Soon you'll be old Jolly Jim again.

I lay down once more and cradled my hero in my arms.

Up the Golden Years

I was back in Rick's office. Our family doctor seated himself behind his desk and rifled the papers he had taken from the voluminous Backus files. Since I had been Rick's patient for some thirty-five hypochondriacal years, they were thicker than *War and Peace.* Thirty-five years! Come to think of it, on my first visit Rick had still been in his naval uniform. He still looked great! Handsome. Fit. No wrinkles. Amazing! The hell it was! It was the back lighting. The crafty old fox! He had arranged his chair so that his back was to the sun and the dancing blue waters of Santa Monica Bay. I sat down. The sun was right in my face. I must have looked like a bas relief map. Next time I'll bring my own gaffer.

We had just come from the examining room where I had undergone my semiannual checkup with all that poking, prodding, and gouging—the blue-plate special. Rick consulted some papers and tapes that had been handed to him by a starched ash-blond nurse who smiled, turned, and crinkled out. Rick leaned back in his chair, causing the sun to diffuse, which gave *him* a dappled patina and at the same time accented *my* liver spots. I wondered if medical school had added lighting to their curriculum along with corporate law and creative bookkeeping.

Rick paused and studied me. His thirty-five years of concern about that battered hulk I call my body was in that look. The sound of an elevator swished up the hall. Muffled *olé*'s emanated from the office of Dr. Alfonso Delgado. Another negative Wasserman! Two ears and a nose!

I sat as Rick studied me, and I listened to the sounds of this formica medical building that I call Andersonville. Any unnecessary moaning and groaning was frowned upon. Save that for the hospital next door! When I had arrived that day I noticed that there had been a change in Andersonville and its satellite, the 640-stall garage. Parking for the handicapped had been reduced from twelve spaces to eight. These, of course, were always occupied by Italian sports cars that were driven by Bruce Jenner look-alikes who jumped out of their Ferraris without ever bothering to open the door. Parking for the handicapped?

Rick indicated the EKG tape he was holding. "Nothing wrong with the ticker. The rest of you checks out as expected. Dr. Muntz assures me your prostate is pretty good for a man of your age. . . . Jim, I'll get down to business. Dr. Ash agrees with Dr. Sawyer. And I go along with them. After studying you for these past five years, we feel now that you *do* have a very slight Parkinson's Syndrome."

"Oh." I brightened. "Like Muhammad Ali?"

He smiled understandingly. He could be a charmer. "It's nothing much, Jim." I gulped. "You see, Jim, you got a pretty bad kick in the ass five years ago when you first got sick, but you weathered it. Now you've got to face the fact that you're older. There are certain changes you'll have to make. We all have to. Nothing drastic. I want to go over your record very carefully, compile a list of do's and don'ts, give you some books on the subject. Next Friday, okay?" I nodded. "Bring Henny with you. Two for one. It's my Friday afternoon special. She may have some questions."

I stared at him. What was Rick getting at? I drove east on Wilshire Boulevard. Come to think of it, four years ago, almost to the day, Rick had laid the basal ganglia on me, and now a safari and three cruises on the Q.E. 2 later (him, not me), I get this Parkinson's Syndrome and geriatric routine. What did he mean, getting old? The best is yet to come. The golden years! Screw the golden years! He sounded like he was reading from a Hallmark card. He'd better have an explanation when I bring Henny in on Friday. Yeah, and how the hell did he think I was going to break getting old to Henny? She didn't even suspect! Was I supposed to walk in and say, "Henny, I'm home! We're old!" How could we be getting old? We never even had a middle age! How could we break it to the neighbors? Actually, I've never seen an old person where we live. What do they do with the old folks? Maybe they took a page from the Eskimos where the old cockers of their own volition walk out into the Arctic night and frappé to death. Maybe they turned them loose on Rodeo Drive with nothing but a Master Card to keep them warm.

There was the sound of a siren. I had gone through that last light on a yellow. The cop stopped his motorcycle. Oh well, I thought, he'll recognize me and I'll just push my "Parking for the Handicapped" sign over to where he can see it. The officer had his book out. "Sorry, officer. About that light . . ." I smiled up at him. He was taking it all in. Finally he put the book back into his jacket. "Look, old fella . . ."

Look, old fella? I was furious!

"I'm going to let you go with just a warning," he continued. "Now get on home while it's still daylight, Grandpa." He got back on his bike and roared off.

Grandpa? The insolence of that kid! I'll call Mayor Bradley! I'll have his badge! As I started the car, I felt as if someone had let the air out of me. Suddenly I *did* feel old. I pulled away from the curb and drove cautiously down

Wilshire. I just wanted to get my ass home. I drove through the Bel Air gates, up the road and into our driveway.

And now I had to break the news to Henny. There she was, standing in the doorway. My God! She was wearing a sheer negligee! What will the neighbors think! Oh, I keep forgetting there are no neighbors where we live. Damn, she was sexier than the first time I ever saw her in a photograph modeling a bathing suit on the cover of a magazine. Now here she was, holding a silver tray on which were standing two rather large martinis. She gave me the high-sign and tossed her head toward the bedroom window, which meant that these were to be imbibed in the privacy of the boudoir. God, how I love her. I could hardly wait.

Well! La dee dah! Screw it! We'll get old tomorrow!